3—

D1277634

The Empty Chair

Love and Loss in the Wake of Flight 3407

𝓛𝓛𝓛𝓛𝓛

ଯୟୟୟୟ

The Empty Chair

Love and Loss in the Wake of Flight 3407

Edited by Gunilla Theander Kester

and Gary Earl Ross

Published by The Writer's Den

Buffalo, New York

The Empty Chair

Love and Loss in the Wake of Flight 3407

All Rights Reserved © 2010 by Gunilla Theander Kester and Gary Earl Ross

No part of this volume may be reproduced or transmitted in any form or by any means, graphic, electronic, or mechanical, including photocopying, recording, taping, scanning, or by any information storage retrieval system, electronic or otherwise, without the written permission of the publisher or of individual authors and artists, who, past the publication date of this cooperative collection, own all rights to their individual contributions, whether poetry, prose, or graphic, whether under a byline, under a pseudonym, or published anonymously.

Front Cover: "The Empty Chair" by N.Jo Tufts

Back Cover: "Susan's Piano" by Karen Chernick

Photo Credits: All photos were submitted by the authors of the pieces in which they appear. The exceptions are the first responder photos, all taken by Jennifer Lee; the photo of Beverly Eckert, submitted by her family but placed with Theresa Wyatt's poem; the hockey portrait of Madeline Loftus, submitted by her mother but placed with Andy Rajeckas' poem; the photos of Gunilla Theander Kester and Susan Wehle, both taken by Jonah Mink; the photo of Susan Wehle which accompanies "Vignette," taken by Dana Wehle; and the photo of the Susansong pendant, adapted from a traditional design by Rick Ellis.

Published by The Writer's Den

www.garyearlross.com

Printed in the United States of America

ISBN: 978-0-557-28906-6

Lovingly Dedicated to Their Memory

and to the hope that those whose stories
are untold here have been told elsewhere and
may be told also in a future edition of this book.

Beverly Eckert, 57
Alison Des Forges, 66
Madeline Loftus, 24
Ellyce Kausner, 24
Jerome Krasuski, 53
Susan Wehle, 55
Don McDonald, 48
Zhaofang Guo, 55
Gerry Niewood, 64,
Coleman Mellett, 34
Mary "Belle" Pettys, 50
David M. Borner, 49
Lorin Maurer, 30
Jean Srnecz, 59
Clay Yarber, 62
Kevin Johnston
John G. Roberts III, 48
Ronald Gonzalez, 44 (Canada)
Beth Ann Kushner, 19
Nicole Korczykowsk
Ronald D. Davidson, 66
Linda C. Davidson, 61
Dawn Mossop
Donald Mossop
Shawn Mossop, 12 (son of Dawn and
Donald Mossop)

Ferris Reid (sister of Dawn Mossop)
Brad Green, 53
Darren Tolsma
Chief Master Sgt. John Fiore, (ret.), 59
Jennifer Neill, 34
Mary Julia Abraham, 44
George Abu-Karem (Israel)
Larry Beutel
Steve Johnson
Kevin Johnston
Ruth Harel Katz
Brian Kuklewicz
Sean Lang
Dawn Monachino
Johnathan Perry
Julie Ries
Kristin Marie Safran, 37
Ernest West, 55
Shibin Yao (China)
Douglas C. Wielinski, 61, (Clarence
homeowner)
Marvin Dean Renslow, 47
Rebecca Lynne Shaw, 24
Matilda Quintero, 57
Donna Prisco
Joseph Zuffoletto, 27

ঞঞঞঞঞ

ଽଽଽଽଽ

CONTENTS

ᘔ ᘔ ᘔ ᘔ ᘔ

𝄞𝄞𝄞𝄞𝄞

Foreword

It was May 14, 2009. Buffalo was dressed in her best spring colors. All of her trees showed new green leaves and her gardens were full of pink, white, and yellow flowers. It was my friend's birthday. I drove to a local supermarket to buy her flowers. Back in January, on the 28th, she had surprised me with flowers on my birthday, a small lovely bouquet of tulips were delivered that afternoon. It was an unusual gesture. She was way too busy and too involved to bother with trivial things like that, so I treasured it all the more. I had just returned from a trip to LA, and she was going off for two weeks of vacation in Costa Rica. On January 30th she sent me an email: "I'm going out of town tomorrow for almost 2 weeks. Sorry I'll miss your reading. Hope your LA trip was great."

I found a bouquet of colorful flowers and joined the line at the cash register. It was lunchtime, and the line was quite long. In front of me were two older ladies. You know the kind of ladies who, in their eighties, seem indestructible, full of energy, and with too much make-up on their leathery skin. One of them turned to me and asked me about the flowers.

"They are for my friend," I said. "Today is her birthday."

They nodded wisely.

"You will give them to her?"

"She gave me flowers on my birthday back in January, so I will give her flowers on hers."

They nodded some more.

"They can arrest me if they want," I added defiantly, wondering what my two daughters would do if I called them from prison.

"Arrest you?" The other old lady was curious.

"My friend died in Flight 3407," I said. "I am taking my flowers to the crash site."

Something momentous and unexpected happened then. All the people who were in line ahead of me stood aside—a communal gesture of respect and grief! I hesitated, but the old lady in front of me grabbed my left arm with steely strength and looked me in the eye: "Now, you take all your good memories with you," she said. "All your good memories!"

And I did.

Leaving the store I thought: only in Buffalo! This is such a unique community. As a friend of mine, a native Buffalonian, put it: "We care for each other here."

Sitting in my car in the parking lot, I could still feel the old woman's hand on my arm, see her dark, painted eyes, and hear her voice. Maybe, I thought. Maybe in some small way we could help each other with our grief? We are all mourning in deeply personal ways and to different degrees, but we are all grieving. That was the simple beginning of this project, and it took root on the road out to Clarence and at the empty place on Long Street where I left my flowers.

I knew I could not do it on my own, so I called Gary Earl Ross. He had recently released a lovely book on a very different topic involving over 50 local writers and poets. Maybe we could do something similar for and about the victims of Flight 3407? Gary was supportive from the start.

Since the tragedy was so recent and an open wound to so many family members and friends, we waited until September to release a call for submissions. By Thanksgiving we knew we had an unusual problem on our hands: Almost all the submissions we had received were dedicated to Cantor Susan Wehle. There were at least two clear reasons for this. On the one hand, Cantor Wehle was a public figure in Buffalo and beyond. Through her work and her life, she had touched so many people's lives. Also, many people who knew Susan knew of our CD and the work we had done together; they trusted that bond. Everywhere I went I heard stories about her. It was wonderful and awful at the same time! But slowly the word of the anthology began to spread, and we started to receive submissions for and about many of the other wonderful people who perished that night. It is with a mixture of deep gratitude and an irrevocable feeling of loss that I dedicate these pages to all the victims of Flight 3407, and to their families and friends.

These pages are what we hope will be a First Edition of an ongoing project. I trust that in another year or two, we will be able to produce a larger, more inclusive edition. As I write these words, only eleven months have passed since that terrible night of February 12, 2009. I know of many people who cannot yet speak about it, let alone write about it. Maybe by reading the words of others, they can begin the long road toward what Susan called Refuah v'Tikvah or "Healing and Hope."

Gunilla Theander Kester
January 12, 2010

Note: I would like to thank Gary Earl Ross for his kindness, skill, and generosity, as well as N.Jo Tufts and Bruce Corris for the final title. I am grateful to my family— Daniel, Anya, and Shiri—for their support, and treasure my special friends Theodora Annas-Strauss and Diane Pontikos, as well as Susan's sisters, Eva and Dana, who "adopted" me. I don't know how I would have gotten through this year without them.

A Second Foreword

On February 12, 2009, I went to bed with mixed emotions. Earlier, at a charity event, I had met an intriguing woman and made arrangements to take her to dinner. My head swam with curiosity about her until I got home and turned on the television. Then I was gripped by the story of Flight 3407, unfolding a short distance from my house near the University at Buffalo South Campus. When finally I put my head on the pillow, the hope inspired by meeting Tammy struggled with the horror of disaster. I had no way of knowing Tammy would become my partner or that, a year later, I would be part of a book about the tragedy then still flashing on the insides of my eyelids.

At three a.m. my phone rang. The call was from my daughter Madelynne, then a student at Buffalo State, who said, through tears, "I think Candi was on that plane." Before I could begin to comfort her about the loss of a roommate, she screamed, "All those people! It's not fair! It's just not fair!" I could hear others around her, also crying. Her boyfriend, she said, was just staring at the TV in shocked silence. "Why do things like this happen?" she cried. "Why?" In all my years as a father and teacher, I never felt more useless than when I replied, "We don't know why they happen. We can't know."

The next morning she called back to say Candi had taken a different flight. Still Maddy couldn't help repeating, "All those people." I told her we didn't have to know them to grieve for them, that they were important to others and their lives deserved to be honored, that while those closest to the victims were affected more than the rest of us this was a community tragedy.

A few days later I heard from my friend Gunilla that her friend Cantor Susan Wehle had been on 3407. Shortly after that I heard from my longtime friends Linda and Amrom that their friend Cantor Susan Wehle had been on the plane. I wondered if Gunilla and Daniel attended the same temple as Linda and Amrom. I asked Linda if they knew each other. They didn't. "But Susan knew a lot of people," I think Linda said.

Over the next week or so I began to hear from others I knew who knew someone aboard the plane—several from UB (where I work) or Buff State or the WNY education community who knew Alison Des Forges, musicians who knew Gerry Niewood, someone who knew Beverly Eckert or Maddy Loftus or Doug Wielinski, the Clarence resident killed on the ground, in his own home. The fine filaments that bind us into a community helped us all feel the tug and pull of that community's pain. Never having been the site of an air tragedy of this magnitude, Western New York was indeed reeling from a shared tragedy, a shared loss.

Several months passed before Gunilla came to me with the idea for this book. A widely published and well respected poet and scholar, she had never before compiled an anthology and worried that the task might be too ungainly for one person, especially one so personally involved. She asked if I would help, if my website, which has evolved into a small independent press, would consider publishing. The purpose of such a book, she said, was not to demand answers of the airline or changes to improve air safety. Those matters would be handled by others. *Love and Loss*, the working title she chose, was to be an act of remembrance, a means for those affected by the tragedy to express their emotions and address their loss. This is the perfect place for this book, she said. With the outpouring of grief, the efforts to help first responders, and the massive internet petition to get a TV network to rebuild the Wielinski home, it was clear that Buffalo and its people are special.

That specialness was reinforced for me in September when a traffic accident claimed the life of Asa Hill, the seven-year-old son and grandson of very dear friends. Away on family business, Tammy and I missed Asa's memorial service but the day after we got back I went to the home of his grandmother, Ujima Theater founder and artistic director Lorna C. Hill. With tears in her eyes Lorna described for me a memorial service that drew 700 people into a church designed to seat 400 and left another 300 or so on the lawn to listen to the service on speakers. "People ask me why I stay in Buffalo," Lorna said. "That's why." And when I got home that day, there was a card from Gunilla, extending her deepest sympathy to me and my "Ujima family"—Asa's mother Rahwa is the theater's executive director, his father Amilcar is the technical director, and I am a resident playwright.

Yes, Buffalo is special, and we are all connected.

In a September reading we did together at the Center for Inquiry, Gunilla and I issued the first official call for manuscripts for this book. Those in attendance agreed to spread the word, and we distributed the call through emails as well as print. The work came in slowly at first, but the pace quickened as we neared our deadline. While most of the submissions were about Susan Wehle, who touched so many lives in Western New York, pieces about others who were lost came in too. Moreover, there were submissions from people who knew no one aboard the plane but nevertheless were affected by the disaster. Meanwhile, Rachel Fix Dominguez was compiling statements about Alison Des Forges and agreed to let part of her yet unfinished *Alison's Book* be included here.

Even in its grief, the work presented in this book is largely positive, with little in the way of anger and much that celebrates the lives of the victims. We honor them all here. It is in recognizing all their lives meant that we find the first threads of peace. It is in the certainty that they would want us to continue living that we can continue living. Ultimately, *The Empty Chair: Love and Loss in the Wake of Flight 3407* is reflective, reverent, loving, and hopeful.

I am honored and humbled to have been a part of its assembly.

Gary Earl Ross
January 12, 2010

First Words

Gunilla Theander Kester

(For Susan)

These were the first words
I read this morning
straight out of *Torah*:

"The Lord said to me:
'Get yourself a large sheet
and write on it in common script
and call reliable witnesses'." (Isaiah, 8)

So I clap my hands, once and loud
call my dead friends, light
a fire and pull a blank page
from an old book. You loved me
although you knew me.

These are the first words
I write tonight.

Sympathetic Grounding

Jane Sadowsky

[Birdwatchers in Western New York observed few birds in the air on a particular Friday in February.]

The birds didn't fly on Friday.
I know; I looked for them.
I wanted to see wings that stayed aloft,
that ferried their passengers safely
from tree to tree.

The birds didn't sing on Friday.
In vain, I listened for them.
I wanted to hear sweet warbling,
to drown out the sirens in my head

The flowers didn't bloom on Friday.
Though February, I searched for them.
The rose that opened to the night air,
had petals of flame.
Its scent lingers.

The empty spaces grow large and larger,
empty seats, empty hands,
empty hearts.

The earth, charred beneath our feet,
swallows our hopes.

The embroidery threads have broken;
the hoop spills.

Long, it will be, and long,
before we can talk of this
without tears.

The birds didn't fly on Friday.
Like our hearts, stilled.

The Music in My Heart

Alexa Draman

My beloved Cantor
I call you my mentor
You sang like a bird
Which still can be heard
Cantor Susan Wehle

Your smile lit up a room
Your laugh carried a tune
Caring, loving, bright
Fill my thoughts at night
Cantor Susan Wehle

Your songs of healing
Leaving the ill feeling
Hope for tomorrow
Hearts filled with sorrow
Cantor Susan Wehle

Your job here has ended
Our hearts will be mended
It now seems more clear
I must wipe my tear
Cantor Susan Wehle

Lots of loving laughter
Remembering after
Our wonderful friend
Why must it all end ?
Cantor Susan Wehle

In heaven you must be,
Sharing songs happily
Healing will soon start
Music in my heart
Cantor Susan Wehle

Airport Encounter

Elizabeth Wheat

I don't know who left the plastic box of cookies on the table in the Juan Santamaria National Airport in Costa Rica. In my early morning foggy state I noticed them only as trash obscuring my clear path to breakfast. Pushing them aside I sat down to enjoy my hash browns and coffee.

Having spent the last month in Costa Rica I was used to seeing words in foreign languages; however, as I digested my breakfast I realized that on the box of cookies the lettering was not in Spanish but in Hebrew. While I pondered why someone would leave a perfectly good looking box of cookies sitting on the table in a busy airport in a country with so few Jewish people, I figured that the cookies must have come from America—why leave so many uneaten on the table?

Another woman moved closer and sat down across from me but closer to the uneaten box of cookies. She was obviously interested in them as well. She seemed to be studying the box with interest born of comprehension and she wondered out loud—why leave a box of organic oatmeal cookies uneaten on the table? She read the Hebrew and learned that they were not just oatmeal, but organic oatmeal cookies! I asked her how she learned to read Hebrew . . .

In the ensuing hour long conversation we shared intimate details of our lives. We also discovered that the box of cookies was left uneaten because it had bugs! She spoke of her sons and told me the importance of respecting children. She described that she hoped to help organize parents and give them more tools to raise loving healthy children. She said that there needed to be more people in the world who "had their shit together!" If the world had more people who knew themselves better she believed then the world would be a better place.

She told me a funny story of her mother—quoting her mom in some European accent foreign to me. In that quote Suzie remembered that when a man's penis is up his head is down! Through that story I learned her first name, but she did not know mine. I smiled at the story and was glad she had shared it with me. I told her of my parents and how they came to understand me as a young lesbian. I told her about how happy they were that my partner and I were about to have a baby—their first grandchild.

In an airport you have a rare opportunity to share yourself with a stranger. You will never see that person again. The usual boundaries are changed. But it isn't everyone you meet in an airport who is interested in engaging. In fact it is the rare case when you find someone interested in sharing, questioning, and listening. In Suzie I found a like-minded woman who shared with me advice on raising conscientious, self-aware sons. I shared stories of my childhood and my hopes for the life of the child my partner and I are about to have. She told me about the recent wedding she had officiated for her niece. She was interested in knowing how the laws worked in Washington State and how long it would take for me to become the adoptive parent of our child.

Thursday morning in the airport I met a woman who freely shared herself with me. That was special. I wonder who else she met as she traveled home. She took time to make a connection with me. I am a soul who now carries some of her stories and I feel blessed by the sharing she made. If her plane had not crashed my thoughts about her would be recorded in a journal—I would never have bothered to look her up online, but she would exist in my writing. Now she exists only in memory and writing. How strange, how lucky and how wonderful it is to bravely welcome newcomers into your life until the very last moment—which, indeed, one does not know when will come.

Missing

Gunilla Theander Kester

(For Susan)

After nine months I venture out
again reborn a new person alone
No longer looking for you, I sit
in the cafe my back to the door
thinking: Why doesn't somebody
call to ask for the old lady with sad
lines in her face sitting all alone
with her back to door and windows
sipping black coffee writing nothing
in her blank notebook. Tell her
please to leave. Nobody will come.
The one she loves is already home.

Gunilla and Susan

Dear Ernie

Jennifer West

Ernie, the moment I met you at work at the printer and you asked me if there were any quicker printers around, then proceeded to tell me (in great detail) the phenomenal presentation you were working on and how you were the best . . . I knew you were *the one*.

Instantly I fell in love—your passion, excitement, and zest for life and your work were inspiring. Your twinkling, beautiful blue eyes (which our daughter has, too) captivated me, along with your optimism, humor, laughter, and smiles...which were all contagious. You were my protector, my security, my savior, my best friend, my soul mate and my world. You never showed me a bad day and always made me feel better when I was overwhelmed. You always took care of Summer and me, while taking on way too much for yourself without one complaint. I've never seen anyone function so well and be so happy on such few hours of sleep. You were so dedicated, I was in awe of you and so very proud of you...you were the best in the business and in your class.

I waited so long for you to come into my life. We had it all, the whole fairytale. It's not fair and I don't understand why you were taken from us. We had so many plans, we were so excited to watch Summer grow and experience being a kid again (although we were already big kids ourselves). Who will I watch Jerry Springer with and go with to our movie marathons? Who will I dance with all night at the disco? Who will watch with me as Summer grows up and help me teach her about life? Who will I act silly with and try terribly to sing with? Who will I barbeque with and swim alongside under the stars? Who will help me carry on traditions? Who will I cry to, talk to, laugh with, cuddle with? The answer was you. But, my saving grace is the best gift you could ever have given me, our beautiful daughter, Summer. She is the everlasting reality of our love. I see so much of you in her. I promise I will never, ever let her forget you and I will let her know how she was the love of your life. I now know why I have so many photo albums and videos of you and her, and us. She will always know you were the best Daddy and the best husband in the world. She will also know how gentle, kind, patient, caring, intelligent, witty, and funny you were. And how many lives you touched. And how you saved her and me when she was born during the October storm. You were our hero and my rock.

Ernie, you are woven into every piece of our home and land. Every flower, bulb, tree, bush and garden you thoughtfully picked out and planted. The deck you built, the pool you designed, the provider you were. Summer will grow up in our home knowing you are here forever. I promise you that.

I love you and miss you so much, you took a piece of me with you. My heart breaks when I look at Summer, knowing she will never see you again. You would be so proud of our family and friends who have supported me so greatly. I am blessed to have them. I just pray you will send me some of your strength so I can be strong for Summer.

Although she's only two, I know she would say this to you:

Daddy, I loved going to Perkins with you every weekend, to the mall, shopping, even Home Depot was fun! I loved going to the garden nurseries with you, to the movies, to the amusement parks and you taking me for all my haircuts. I loved riding the John Deere with you, swimming with you, sharing ice cream, cereal and cookies with you. I loved riding real high on your shoulders while playing the tambourine, getting horsey rides and how you made me laugh all the time. I loved your kisses as you tucked me in bed and read me books. I loved your cooking (so did Mommy) and your taste in clothes, I love your bright colors. I love how proud of me you were, how much you loved me and how safe you made Mommy and me feel. . . but most of all, Daddy, I love you and you are the best Daddy in the world and Mommy will never let me forget. So, we aren't going to say goodbye, because we know you will always be with us. Now you just have beautiful, safe wings to fly around with as all the best angels do.

1954

Jennifer West

The crisp autumn air breathes your name.

As the tears well up,

I am awakened with warm, nostalgic memories.

Yet broken at the realization that these are all I have left.

I have to bury you again, with my friend at my side.

The finality of the moment births the eternity of our bond.

We will continue to fight, good will prevail.

Why is it death always breathes life?

I look at our child, she has your eyes.

Your tenacity, charm, wisdom.

She has your heart.

A calm, reassuring peace settles me…

She is you.

Until we meet again.

I love you, Ernie.

Journal Excerpts
Jennifer West

May 5, 2009

Today was a rough day. When my Dad and I were outside playing with Summer, I kept thinking how unfair it is that Ernie isn't here to enjoy this and I am. I took pics of Summer standing by the tulips Ernie planted and she picked two for me. She was having so much fun going up the rock wall and down the slide....then I just felt an overwhelming sadness come over me, and guilt. I went in the house and cried... I miss him so much and it's still incredulous to me that he's never coming home. How can I enjoy life when he is not here, he gave me this nice life, the house, and Summer, etc. It's not fair. It was his hard work that got us here and he's not here to enjoy it with us. It really is not fair and I can not accept it.

Anyway, tonight when Summer was sitting on the sink in her bathroom, she had me play the musical mermaid globe (which she never does) that plays "Somewhere Over The Rainbow" (which was one of Ernie and my songs) while she was looking in the medicine cabinet mirror and she said that she has green eyes, (she knows she has blue). Ernie ALWAYS used to tell her how he and she both have blue eyes and Mommy has green eyes. And that blue is prettier, ha ha. Anyway, I told her that she has blue eyes and *I* have green. I usually tell her that she has blue eyes like Daddy's, but I didn't this time, because I didn't want to tear up. . . then she looked at me funny and looked at the mirror. So, I closed the mirror door, thinking we were done. She had me open it back up and stared at her eyes real close and asked, "What are these ?" as she pointed to her eyelashes. I said that they were eyelashes and she asked if I had them and I told her that I did and was blinking. As I was saying that, in my head I was saying to myself that Mommy has little, crappy lashes, and you have Daddy's pretty long lashes.

All of a sudden she said, "Daddy loves you." Then before I could react she said that she loves me, too. I asked her, "Daddy loves me?" And she said, "Yes." I asked if he told her that, and she said, "He says, hi." Then I said, "Daddy told you that at night?" (If I ask her too many questions she clams up and gets embarrassed.) And she said, "No, *Codis* (Daddy's angel friend that is with him apparently) told me." At this point I was trying so hard to hold back my tears but I couldn't, so she got all worried and asked if I was okay. I couldn't stop crying, so I told her that I missed Daddy. I couldn't help it. It was just so weird, because I really was missing Ernie today more than the usual huge amount I do every day. And then she told me that, I mean it came out of nowhere. It was like he told her to tell me that.

June 2, 2009 2:34am
Robin and I had to go to a hearing this morning downtown to prove we were their spouses to get the insurance benefits. Believe that?

Everyone is asking how Summer and I are doing, so I feel I have to be honest and explain exactly what I went through for them to get a better understanding. Friday was an extremely difficult day. Robin and I had to go to the funeral home because we got a call that they identified more "body parts" and they wanted to know what to do with them. We never asked if Ernie and Darren were "all there" when they were cremated, I just knew there was no hair for a locket. So, the phone call shocked us to say the least.

Anyway, they have Ernie's left foot. Against everyone's pleading not to (esp Todd Pacer of the Pacer Funeral home) I asked to see it. I felt like I owed it to Ernie to be there and be with him and be strong, even if it was just his foot, since I couldn't see his body in the beginning. It sounds weird, but I didn't want his foot to feel all alone. It was in a clear baggy and I put on gloves so I could touch it through the baggy. It did not resemble anything like a foot and it was the worst sight I've ever seen. It was charred black, deformed and mushy. But I felt around to try to find his big toe, the one I used to massage when his feet hurt, and I believe I felt it. I saw a bone protruding through the mass. I wondered if that's how his whole body looked or his foot got that way from a few months of sitting there....I'm hoping it's the latter. I also saw 3 vials. One had lung tissue (I think), and the other two had bones. Todd wouldn't leave me alone in the room (I think he was more freaked out than me), until I insisted. I said goodbye to Ernie's foot, said I was sorry I couldn't be there for him or help him and that I loved him, and then I kissed the baggy. Sounds strange, but no matter how gruesome it looked, I didn't want to leave him, because it was my Ernie. It's all I had left. And it didn't seem gruesome to me, nor did I get squeamish, I just kept feeling it, knowing I was touching him. We had to pick out little coffins for them to be cremated in (it's the law that they have to cremate body and parts in a container of some sort) and I am picking out some necklaces with his ashes in it for Summer and other family members, since I didn't realize the first time around that I could get other people necklaces. I have to pick out another urn because mine is sealed and cannot be opened since it is glass and it would shatter. I have to go back to pick all these things out, since I ran out of time at the funeral home to do that.

Summer has been extremely clingy to me. She has seen me crying about this latest tragedy. She says she misses Daddy and asks where he is. She looked at a pic of him and me and said, "That's MY Daddy." She is really afraid she's going to lose me, too.

I feel as if it's February 12 all over again. It seems like there is always something new. June 8th would have been our five-year anniversary. I miss him so much, I miss every little thing. I would give anything to hear his snoring that annoyed me so much before. I still think he's going to walk through the door. The nightmares continue and now I have new ones imagining how his foot got cut off and wondering if he felt it. Would you believe there are some cold-hearted people who say Robin and I should "get over it already"? They have no clue what we are going through and hopefully never will. I lost the love of my life, and Summer lost her Daddy. I didn't get to say goodbye or even see him. I keep imagining how he died and how scared he was. And how I wasn't with him. I have guilt that I'm living and he's not. I have guilt for everything. I am now a single mother responsible for her and myself, for our house, our bills, the yard work, the pool maintenance, food, the creditors, every decision, cleaning, errands, lawyer meetings, benefit meetings, doc appts. All by myself and while taking care of a scared, extremely active two-year-old who attaches to my legs and cries when the phone rings or doorbell rings. I have to try not to cry in front of her. I go to bed alone, I wake up alone. I have no break except at 2am when I am finished with my chores.

Thank God I have wonderful friends and family members that help me when they can. They have gone above and beyond and it cheers me up so to have people here. It really helps (especially Kara and Hannah watching stupid B movies with me, ha ha!) and brightens my day. Yet when everyone leaves and I am alone, it still doesn't make me not miss Ernie. I miss watching The Office with him, going for ice cream, singing and dancing with him, sharing our pride over Summer with him, acting like goofballs together, our cute little sayings to each other. Every time Summer does something cute (which is a lot) I always think, "Oh, I have to tell Ernie what she did today." And I go to pick up the phone or I think I can't wait to tell him when he gets home from work. All my dreams are shot. He was going to show Summer and me the world. We were going to take her to Disney, to Italy, to Australia, to Maui for our 5th anniversary, and it's all gone. I don't have the travel savvy that he did to take her myself. We couldn't wait to see her grow, go to school, finally get big enough to go on the big girl rides.....he never heard her say I love you, which she says now. Every place I go, I went with him and it reminds me of him, even Wegmans for grocery shopping!

Every dream and experience was supposed to be shared with him. I am functioning as best as I can and staying strong, but I do not miss him any less and it does not get easier with time. New routines may set in, but it is not easier. In fact it seems harder now. I just am learning to deal better. Spring and summer were Ernie's and my seasons . . . all his bulbs are grown and flowers are blooming. They're all alive from him, but he's not here to enjoy them, and I feel guilty that I am. I miss him so much and it's worse when the weather is nice. I see him all around me. He and Summer are my life, half of my heart was taken with him. Summer was robbed of the best Daddy around and I was robbed of my best friend. My life began when I met him. My heart breaks when she asks, "Where's Daddy?" So, it is hard to just "get over that." I will never get over this. But I will continue to live. And Ernie will live on through me and Summer, and every life he touched. I am staying strong for Summer and Ernie, but sometimes it is hard to find time to just take a breath. It's always go, go, go. But I suppose that's my mind tricking itself into not thinking about the reality.

The Empty Chair

For Susan

In Memoriam

Barbara D. Holender

Is it any comfort to think
there's one more glorious voice
among the heavenly choir?
Something must survive the wasting.

Oh, she was joyous and strong,
full-throated and ardent—
such a soul does not linger.
What goes down in flame
rises in song. We hear her still—

Shiru l'Adonai shir hadash,
Sing, Susan, sing unto the Lord
a new song.

Originally appeared in *Reform Judaism*, Summer 2009

Death is Hard to Write About

Margaret Merrill

You want comfort
reassurance about the beyond,
well worn clichés
about mercy and sleep.

I can say *I'm sorry*
but to go further
requires me to put my fingers
into the holes in your grief

the hole in the holiday
the hole at 5:15
the hole in the white noise
the hole in the ball game
the hole in the kitchen
the hole in your day
the hole in the pew
the holes in the photos
the empty place in your bed
happy birthday replaced by anniversary
a *stop* sign in time.
I can't do this without touching the hole in my own heart.

And then the question chimes in:
Why
can't we keep them with us?
Why
did they have to leave us so soon?

I don't know how
to patch your grief.
I only know how to
bleed mine line by line.

I *do* know how to remind you
of the lesson you've already learned
that you are brothers and sisters
parents and children and friends,
a community walking together
marking graves
with the stones of memories.

A Mother's Letter
Damasa Abraham

Dear Dr. Kester:

I have been contacted by Barbara Miller, who is our cousin, about the anthology book. I will tell you some words about our daughter, Mary Julia Abraham. She was also a passenger on Flight 3407, sitting in row 3, seat C. She was 44 years old on February ninth, three days before the tragedy.

Mary Julia was a witty, happy-go-lucky girl who loved, cared for, and worried about her parents and family and friends. She also cared about the sick and about disabled veterans. As you might have read, her smile and friendliness were contagious. She was returning home that night, from New Jersey, where she had been teaching a disabled vet about his electric wheelchair. That was one of her areas of expertise.

Mary Julia was also an Army Reserves Retiree, an LPN, a respiratory therapist, a greyhound rescuer, and a motorcyclist. She had a very strong faith in her religion.

I miss seeing her walk through my door. I miss her phone calls. Sometimes she called to just go for ice cream, or sometimes she would say, *Mamacita, donde esta mi Papi*, trying out the little Spanish she knew.

My daughter will live forever in our memories.

I am very grateful to you and your colleagues for this opportunity to share. God Bless you all.

Sincerely,

Damasa "Tita" Abraham

The Loss of a Special Person and Special Friend

Jay L. Mesnekoff

Late afternoon on Thursday, February 12, 2009, I received a phone call from Cantor Susan Wehle from the Houston, Texas airport, where she had landed and had a layover on her way home from vacation in Costa Rica. She was awaiting a flight to Newark where she would make a connecting flight back home to Buffalo. She told me she had had a wonderful time in Costa Rica and as always, she was her usual bubbly self.

We discussed many things, including the upcoming hafTorah portion I was reading on Saturday morning at our local, conservative Temple. Saturday, February 14th would be my birthday and I had not read the hafTorah portion at Temple since I had done so at my Bar-Mitzvah, thirty-four years ago. Susan wished me "good luck" in her encouraging way, we then caught up on Temple and business related subjects, shared a few laughs and said our goodbyes.

My house in Clarence Center, New York, is under the normal flight-pattern for planes arriving to the Buffalo International Airport. I am used to hearing the planes overhead; however, on the evening of February 12th, the sounds of a plane overhead sounded much different from any other time before. I heard a high-pitched whining sound from a low, fast-flying plane, that shook my bedroom windows. One of my daughters received a call within minutes of the sound from a friend asking if she was all right since there was a plane that had just crashed in Clarence Center approximately one mile from our home.

The next morning while beginning a funeral service at my funeral home, I received a phone call from Rick Ellis, Executive Director at Temple Beth Am. He was notifying all of the executive board members that our dear friend, Cantor Susan

Wehle, was one of the passengers on Continental Flight 3407. My heart instantly sank.

I was told to come to the Temple as soon as I could. Approximately one hour later I arrived at Temple Beth Am where Rabbi Alex Lazarus-Klein, of Temple Sinai, was waiting with outstretched arms along with other executive board members, wives and staff as we all tried to absorb the devastating news. Rabbi Irwin Tanenbaum, our Rabbi at Beth Am, had just left the day before to go to Arizona and due to the remoteness of his location could not be with us as quickly as he would have wished. Rabbi Tanenbaum and his wife Marta, were able to board flights and be back in Buffalo early Saturday morning and immediately joined the congregation in our shared grief.

On Friday night Rabbi Rosenfeld, of Temple Beth Zion, offered to conduct Shabbat Services with Cantor Barbara Ostfeld, who is the Placement Director of The American Conference of Cantors and a former Cantor at Temple Beth Am. Rabbi Steven Mills, The URJ Regional Director whose office is in Cleveland, Ohio, was also on the bimah, along with all of the executive board members and staff from Temple Beth Am. We started the service with the lighting of the Shabbat candles and led the congregation in the Kiddush. The Temple was filled to capacity.

It was respectful of Continental Airlines to work through our local and state funeral associations to make sure a Jewish Funeral Home was contacted for the handling of the Jewish remains. When it came time to provide my professional services for Cantor Wehle and the other Jewish individuals whom I took care of that perished on Flight 3407, there were extensive protocols set up that had to be followed with the proper sensitivity and competency that they deserved. Working with the various agencies on both the federal and local levels, we made every effort to provide the families with the assistance they needed during this most difficult time.

Sunday evening after meeting with Cantor Wehle's family, we arranged for a Memorial service to be held at Temple Beth Am on Wednesday, February 18th, 2009. Rick Ellis, Executive Director at Temple Beth Am, was instrumental in helping coordinate this service. With permission from the family we arranged a live feed of the service to be transmitted to Temple Sinai in Amherst, NY where Susan had formerly been a Cantor. We also sent live feeds to specific areas in the United States and around the world at the request of the family. A beautiful and moving Memorial Service, filled with song, prayer, personal memories and spirituality was coordinated through the efforts of Cantor Robert Esformes and Linda Hirschhorn, both of the Jewish Renewal Movement and Rabbi Irwin Tanenbaum.

In my funeral business, I have worked professionally with Susan on many services over the years and have always valued her spirituality and her many talents. During the past few years, it had been my pleasure to sing with Susan during concerts, Friday night services and other Temple functions.

Cantor Susan Wehle was a special person. This past summer my Aunt Gail Klein-Davidson was suddenly diagnosed with lung cancer and passed away at the age of sixty two. Susan visited my Aunt Gail and comforted my Aunt with songs and prayers before her death. My Aunt told me that she was incredibly thankful for the time and effort Susan put forth to bring her comfort when she was ailing. She had also shared in many life cycle events for my own family as she had done for so many of the families in our congregation and other congregations. She was a real asset to our Temple family, the community at large and everyone else that she touched. We will miss her effervescent, beautiful smile and her incredible spirit. I will cherish my memories of her forever.

Boat on the Hudson

Gunilla Theander Kester

(For Susan)

How I wish you'd traveled by boat up the salt-mixed Hudson
to old Erie Canal, caressed by air curling your hair into knots
we could've unraveled together, slowly, without words,
east-west, north-south, so that stupid journalist would never
have called me your "pal" and because that's the way to go,

with dignity the way ancient Viking ships carried furs,
slaves and amber. We, too, vessels of warmth, the enslaved,
golden beauty. Going slowly under clouds until coast
gives way to dark mountains, rising shadows
pierced by night fires, pearls scattered among ashes.

Traveling a day or two, a night, or two nights and a day.
Taking your time. Smoke from the boat's chimney lingers
in your hair, mingles slowly, like a man and a woman in love.
Not in a hurry. It's the way to return, early,

before dawn, cold and eager, still wrapped in midnight's
velvet when poets stay, look at stars, trace a word
or two in dew on the railing or in notebooks. Your book
is closed. How I wish you had traveled by boat.

Thoughts of Him Cross My Mind Every Day
Kaylee Kuklewicz

Thoughts of him cross my mind every day,
Questioning God, "Why him? He deserved to stay..."

All we have left of him are the good ol' memories
Vacations, camping, and those hot summer days.

My Uncle Brian was a great father and husband.
He loved his twin sons and wife with all his might.

He had such a great personality; and a laugh that kept us going.
It's going to be hard, but we have each other to keep moving.

He was a travelin' kind of man, that's what he loved to do.
Especially with his family, and business trips too.

He made our family bond stronger than ever.
And helped put the little fights and nonsense behind...

I don't understand why it was his time to go,
He still had a whole life ahead of him, to see his children grow.

What I do know is that he didn't die without a fight,
Because that's my uncle for ya, one strong guy.

Brian Kuklewicz and Family

Angels Near to Him

Marianne Wisbaum

"...God, glory and majesty to Him, does not do things by direct contact. God burns things by means of fire; fire is moved by the motion of the sphere; the sphere is moved by means of a disembodied intellect, these intellects being the 'angels which are near to Him', through whose mediation the spheres [planets] move... thus totally disembodied minds exist which emanate from God and are the intermediaries between God and all the bodies [objects] here in this world." - <u>Guide for the Perplexed</u>, *Maimonides, 11:4 & 11:6*

I just opened two emails from Temple Beth Am, both regarding Cantor Susan Wehle and the tragedy of flight 3407. One email showed a televised news segment of the memorial dedication service that we recently held for Susan and the other was an announcement about this book, asking if any family or friends of the victims would like to send in thoughts or pictures about Susan or any of the other 49 victims of the doomed flight. I immediately emailed Gunilla Theander Kester, whom I have had the honor to work with on Susan's memorial committee, to thank her for doing this book. Up to this point, I had not been able to write down my feelings about Susan or the horrific crash.

The first time our family witnessed Susan's warmth, vibrancy, charm and talent was in 1996, when she was the Cantorial Soloist at a Bat Mitzvah in Temple Sinai. I knew immediately that she was very special. She just lit up the room and got everyone involved. We looked forward to seeing Susan at several other occasions at Temple Sinai in the years that followed. Never did we dream that, years later, Susan would be our Cantor (at Temple Beth Am) and that she would be teaching our own daughter, Arielle, to chant Torah at her Bat Mitzvah. I still remember how welcome and comfortable she made everyone feel, encouraging us to include non-Jewish family members in the service and helping us to assign roles for each of them.

Later that same year, Susan honored Arielle by asking her to chant Torah at Yom Kippur services. I remember how astonished I was that, even with her busy schedule, Susan thought nothing of coming to our home, at times, to teach the lessons. Even though Arielle was quite nervous about chanting in front of the entire congregation,

Cantor Wehle had a way of giving her the calm confidence she needed to look as though she had been doing it for years. Arielle has been honored to do it every year since. This year's service was particularly difficult because of Susan's absence; but somehow, Arielle chanted as if Susan was right there by her side. (We would like to believe that she **was** there by her side, and that she was smiling her broad, trademark smile!)

Rather fittingly, Rabbi Tanenbaum's sermon at that service was about angels. "Do Jews believe in angels?" the rabbi asked. The rabbi explained that Jews, in fact, do believe in angels, proving his point by citing several examples from Torah and saying that he has met several people in his life who he feels are angels. Susan, also, believed in angels. She sang about them on the beautiful, "Songs of Healing & Hope" CD that she did with Gunilla. Being raised Catholic, I have believed in angels for as long as I can remember, but it is not a topic that comes up very much in temple or with my Jewish friends and family. So, I went to my computer to find out more about angels and Judaism. I found the following definition of angels: *"Angels are spiritual beings found in many religious traditions. They are broadly viewed as messengers of God, sent to do God's tasks."*

I also found listings of various angels, but one stuck out to me as an angel that was very near and dear to Susan's heart: *Shekinah* (or *Shekhina*). The definition that I found of Shekinah is: *"the angel of unity and unconditional Love . . . Shekinah inspires us to be fair, bringing balance and harmony to our entire being."*

Susan sang about Shekinah with such joy in her heart. She was all about unity and unconditional love. She welcomed people of all cultures and faiths and she made everyone feel very special and loved. One of the reasons that we miss her so much is because she had such a fierce sense of fairness and justice and she inspired so many with her full-out smile, her encouraging words and her beautiful voice. Just being in her presence brought *balance* and *harmony*, even on a chaotic day.

Since that plane fell out of the sky on that cold February night, there have been constant reminders about it in every major media outlet. The reminders, though they have been necessary and helpful in some ways (the most important of which is to try to make flying safer) have also served to keep the deep wounds of loss and grief open for the friends and families of the victims. As I have tried to make some sense of it all, I have often wondered how God could let things like this happen. But, in the process of writing about Susan and the overall impact of the lives lost, I am beginning to understand, with the help of the quote from Maimonides at the beginning of this piece.

I did not personally know everyone who perished in the blaze. The only one I knew personally was Susan Wehle. However, I have some personal friends who knew some of the others and after having read most of the biographies, it is apparent that there were many extraordinary people whose lives were snuffed out when that plane plunged to earth in fiery flames.

God burns things by means of fire, fire is moved by the motion of the sphere;
the sphere is moved by...'angels that are near to Him.' [from Maimonides, above]

Maybe all God's creations are fashioned to interact in a particular order, with a particular sense of 'balance and harmony.' What may appear on the surface to us to be chaos, or evil could, upon further inspection, be all part of the natural order of things. If we have faith in God's supreme power and goodness, and we believe that angels exist as messengers of God, then we can once again find a sense of balance and harmony, even after our most traumatic and sorrowful losses.

We can go on living because we have faith that, indeed, God and angels do exist...angels we have known and angels we are yet to know. Ancient writings are full of wisdom that transcends time. Susan, and perhaps many of the other flight victims, showed us how to live joyfully and peacefully, with full-out smiles. Susan welcomed unity, loved unconditionally, and advocated for equality and justice. Now, the angels have completed the tasks that God gave them. They have left us with such a great legacy to carry forth.

Over the years, I have had the honor and pleasure of working on various committees that Susan was a part of. She was always a delight to be with because she had so much positive energy. The last time I saw her, it was only for a fleeting few moments at the temple office. Looking back, I wish I had spoken to her longer and given her a hug. But I was in a hurry.

If I could speak to Susan now, I would say thank you to her for being such an inspiration to our whole family—and I would give her a big hug. To her family and to the families of the other victims, we send our deepest sympathies and hugs.

We hope that you find some comfort in the lovely verse that we used at Arielle's Bat Mitzvah. It was one of Susan's favorites and we feel that it describes the way she 'walked (and sang) through life.' Peace, love, hope and joy to all of you.

A Blessing for My Daughter (by Myrna Rabinowitz)

May you walk through life as a person.
With other people, with other people,
May you walk through life as a person,
Kind and just and caring.
May you walk through life as a woman.
With other women, with other women.
May you walk through life as a woman,
Proud and strong and sharing.
May you walk through life as a sister
And a daughter and a mother
May you walk through life as a sister
Nurturing and giving
May you walk through life with Shekhina
Guiding you, guiding you.
May you walk through life with Shekhina
And know the joy of living.

Grief: Flight 3407

Linda Hirschhorn

what do you do when the accidental death
comes your way
a father
a best friend
and yet again

one death brings up another

you sit and wait
wait for more news
where was she coming from
why that flight
when is the funeral
how are the boys

Susan and Linda

i worry about the etiquette of tragedy
is it ok to eat chocolate
play scrabble
make love
what kind of person even thinks about such things
at such a time

the crash was on the news the night before
better check in with her
of course i'm ok she would say
don't worry about me
you trip over remorse
you hadn't talked in so long
you stumble into magical thinking
go back to bed
declare a do-over
make the news go away

better yet

call her now
because she would be the one to call in times like these
ask about her headaches
was the trip to Costa Rica amazing
what new songs are you teaching

soon we would laugh
our deep belly laughs
an hour would pass
we'd hang up
only partly filled
by long distance connection

(here is what's true
the I i was
with you
died too)

a friend has written
'Susan is an amazing soul
may her travels in mystery be the most holy of callings'

'Is.'

can i imagine her floating
gazing with astonishment
at all the souls
who've come to welcome her
already she is rushing into our dreams
to comfort us in song

Through Fire and Ice
In Memory of Beverly Eckert (1951-2009)

Theresa Wyatt

After the box cutter
September horror
of smoke and fear

when a new century collapsed
in less than two hours,

after an ordinary cell phone
communicated

last loving words to you

through what must have been
behemoth grief,

you set about a course to make
breathing precious again

My silence cannot be bought,
and to those who mongered war,
Not in my name, you said

and after smoke and ash
permeated every corner
of our vulnerable cities

you turned universal facts
of grief and consequence
into revelations

with seamless conviction
and passionate pleas

through panels and hearings,
and endless reports,

prodding ways forward truthfully
into a language of justice and peace,

necessary still
and likely to always be so,

these true ways forward
like that cold winter night
full of fire and ice

when you sailed skyward
toward binary stars

and the harvest of your life blended
with the model of your soul
illuminating everything
still moving
beneath it

Strong Woman

Margot Eckert

(From Beverly Eckert's Memorial Service, February 21, 2009)

My little girl sister
> could out bike, out dodge ball, and out hide and seek the
> neighborhood gang,
> fort building, tree climbing, cowboy hat and Cisco Kidding,
> mouseketeering, red wagoneering
> jump roping, hop scotching,

Playground pal, was my little girl sister.

My Teenager sister
> granny glasses, peasant dresses,
> Buffalo Academy of Sacred Heart classes,
> one act plays,
> hot uniforms all day
> spit curls, bangs, CYO
> basketball games,
> transistor radio
> Canisius dances, Sean Rooney romances
> waitressing and babysitting,

Beatlemaniac, was my teenage sister.

Art woman, my sister
> portrait painting
> sketches, drawing
> pottery making from shapeless slabs of heavy clay

up the stairs dragging, across the floors sagging

sitting on her stool, wheel spinning, iron fingers shaping,

kiln firing

Talent abounds in my AllenTown Arts Festival sister.

Music woman, my sister

    piano and guitar playing

    Bach loving, Ella Fitzgerald adoring

    tap dancing

    voice singing

    harmonies humming

    birthday lyrics composing

Clapping and performing from my music sister.

Fun woman, my sister

    kayaking

    tubing

    sailing

    swimming

    snorkeling

    skiing

    hiking

    biking

Beverly and her siblings

    watch out! - roller   blading

    mountain climbing

    book clubbing

    niece and nephew trip taking

    Neverland Island hopping

    world traveling- Paris, Italy, London, Mexico, Morocco

Disney World

the theatre world

to concerts

and restaurants

Cove Beach picnics

On the go fun, with my motion sister.

Kitchen woman, my sister

    big wooden table, guests surrounding

    chopping, slicing, mixing, spicing,

    broiling, baking, pasta rolling,

    feasting, laughing, drinking,

    toasting to family, friends and neighbors,

Soul nourishing... making meals with my kitchen sister.

Garden woman, my sister

    lush lawn, stone walks,

    clematis run amok

    dinosaur sized Rhododendrons,

    hydrangea heaven

    grass mower, leaf raker,

    dirt shoveler, ground shaper

Landscapes sculpted by my garden sister.

Builder woman, my sister

    renovations big and small

    fixing ceilings

    pipes

    walls

    wires

stucco and stone steps

windows and doors, hardware stores,

Eggertsville, Breckenridge, Enfield, Easton, Elizabeth, then

Stamford

her home...Katrina homes... Habitat homes...into our homes,

Always feel at home with my builder sister.

Strong woman, my sister

asking questions

getting answers

pushing governments

prodding presidents

speaking justice

lobbying, persuading

impatient staring, locked gaze, glaring

reading, researching, pondering, believing

tenacious—when tired

nonsense not tolerated

email queen

determined, never mean

The Infomatrix... don't mess with my sister.

Strong woman, my sister

Now your sister too

World's sister

Body stilled

Spirit NOT killed . . . of this good sister

Spirit now STRONGER . . . pay it forward much longer

With us... within us... our sister lives still.

A Mother's Remembrance

Anna Marie Russo

Madeline Loftus was my oldest daughter. She was 24 and meant the world to her family and friends.

Madeline enjoyed her life and had such an exciting bright future ahead of her. She had worked her way through college but always found time to volunteer to help others. She moved back home to New Jersey to be closer to her family and to start a promising career in a top pharmaceutical advertising firm. She was absolutely thrilled to work there beside team members who loved and respected her. Somehow she found time to coach a junior high school age traveling hockey team. Last winter she would leave work every afternoon and play ice hockey out on an open pond.

You see, she had been the only girl on the high school hockey team, and her love of the game had kept her busy every day, as an active player on travel teams. She had gone on to play college ice hockey for Buffalo State and then, after moving to Minnesota, for St. Mary's University.

She was so full of life, and took part in everything life had to offer. Her motto was *live, laugh, love!* The fun Madeline had with her brother, sister, and friends was priceless. In addition to hockey, she loved skiing, hiking, traveling, the beach, fishing, and sushi and always found time for her friends, traveling all over to make sure she spent time with everyone, even those who lived away from where she was. On February 12, 2009 she was on her way to Buffalo State to spend the weekend with her college friends and to play ice hockey at what was supposed to be a reunion game. For weeks she told everyone she came in contact with how much fun she anticipated. Even though she had gone skiing in Vermont two weekends in January, and New Hampshire in the beginning of February, the excitement of playing hockey with her friends made her happier than anything.

Now she is skating with the stars in heaven, and we all miss her so much.

Message from Maddy

Andy Rajeckas

The brightest light doesn't always last
Good times go by too fast.
Summer won't stay for long
You can't always get to hear the whole song

I wish I could've of been here longer
But now it's time for me to move on
I feel such peace and serenity
It's so much more than I would've known.

I'm skating with the stars
I'm scoring goals from Venus to Mars.
I'm a bird, I'm an angel, I'm the wind blowing free
Just look in your heart... you'll find me

Listen to what I will say
Please don't cry, 'cause I'm okay.
Just keep me in your memories
Let's dance again in a summer breeze.

Be true to yourself, be all you can be
I hope that's how you'll remember me.
If you want an answer, if you need a sign
Just live your life the way I lived mine . . .

I'm skating with the stars

I'm scoring goals from Venus to Mars,

I'm a bird, I'm a rainbow, I'm an angel set free

Just look in your heart, you'll find me

I'm skating with the stars

I'm scoring goals from Pluto to Mars!

I'm a bird, I'm a rainbow, I'm an angel set free

Just look in your heart, you'll find me . . .

Thank you Mom for all that you've done

Thank you Dad for days in the sun

Thanks, my family, I know how you cared . . . thanks my friends, for the times that we shared . . .

I'm skating with the stars . . . '.Just scored three goals, from Venus to Mars . . .

The Empty Chair

54

Go Now to Your Streetness
Gunilla Theander Kester
(For Susan)

Go now to your sweet streetness;
I stand here and spit on the sidewalk.

Last night you threw pebbles from your window
I went back and picked up every one.

Walls you rest on or climb over, you said,
but I am running right into this one. Again
and again. Crush my mouth open.

I at the side of the street when you walked by,
stopped, put your hand on my foot,
rested there, looked at me on my ladder, hand still
stretched toward the light bulb I meant to change.

Before you even stopped
I renamed your street. And mine.

Like Jacob with my ladder, *I'll carry*
that weight, carry that weight
a long time.

When you came walking down that ugly street,
I on a wobbly ladder trying to fix my streetlight,

dogs barked. Toothless women smacked their lips.
Old men remembered to whistle. Young girls
lifted their skirts higher. Cars screeched mercy.

An evening blue and smooth like a moon
of unrest. Letters of need. Signs of desire.
Every thing has its color.

Folly me, thought I could keep you.
Folly me, thought you'd walk by.
Like Hamlet, *I have of late, wherefore*
I know not, lost all my mirth.
Except I know why, I know, I know.

Worn out by disease and poverty.
Worn out, already, by tomorrow
when you stopped by my ladder
counted the bones in my foot.

Calls of protests, warnings
scribbled on walls, buses,
poems, names
of those arrested, killed:
Our Book of the Dead.
Our Lexicon of Grief.

Our Alphabet of Woe.
Who by water and who by fire?

Mine all texts now, no matter age or origin!

Imagine all the people
living for today
Except one, except one.

Grief and fury pull me into brutal beauty.
On porches, in golden palaces, they scatter
hard pearls everywhere; their street the blade
of a sharp knife, a shard of polished glass
cuts through my cheek a new mouth. What will it
say? Known to river gods and ghosts looking
 for their shape. I am beside myself. There I
will wait for my return. In song. In psalm.
This is how angels die. Outside. Each alone.
Darkness starts where day begins.

Beside myself, a sister I never had,
 a mother who spoke one word.

Sprinkle my broken house with salt.

Susan, Our Friend

N.Jo Tufts

Our friends are the family we get to choose.

> They don't love us "unless..," or "until..." or "as long as…"
>
> They love us when they think we're right and when we're not even close.

Susan has been our friend.

Our friends demand little of us.

> They don't expect us to pay their bills,
>
> Raise their children,
>
> Take care of their relatives
>
> Or do their laundry. They simple love us.

Susan has been our true friend.

Friends cry with us, and laugh with us,

> and laugh *at* us,
>
> and share with us,
>
> and listen to us.

Susan has been a friend to all of us, here.

With our real friends we feel safe,

> to reveal our deepest, truest selves,
>
> to discover who we are,
>
> and what we're not,
>
> and what we can be, if we dare.

Susan was so good at being our friend.

For those blessed to truly walk with God,

strangers are just friends they haven't met yet,

    and so for Susan, that made this world a very friendly place, indeed.

She wanted, more than anything, to walk this life with God.

    Who's to say, it may have been this very strong desire the drew her from us

        at this young age.

    She did more in each day, each week, each year, than any other human we

    have known. I can tell you this because there are six of us now trying to cover

    the responsibilities she handled at Temple Beth Am, and we are struggling.

It's hard to know how to mourn a friend while we still try so hard to work.

It's hard to work when our hearts are aching,

    when we miss her radiant smile in every moment,

        every meeting, every service.

Today, the Friendship sails on winds of change,

    and nothing will ever be the same again, for any of us.

    But when grief fades, love remains.

    Love never dies.

Our love for our friend and her love for all of us,

    now freed from the mortal body where it once dwelled,

    fills our own hearts— all of us and all of you and, I believe,

        surrounds and fills this precious world we call our home.

    More, even, than the air we breathe, love sustains us, even in our sadness.

    Let this love also remain with us in easier days sure to come,

        and guide each of us, like our dear sweet friend,

        who never asked for much, but hoped for this:

        for each of us to be a blessing in our own way

            to keep the circle whole.

Epiphany 6 – from Trinity/ St. John Lutheran Church, February 14/15, 2009

Pastor Peter Breitsch

On Friday morning, after my bus run, I was watching the events surrounding the crash of Flight 3407, and I heard Governor Paterson's words at the news conference with Chris Collins. One line in his speech was: "We try to love our neighbor as we love ourselves, but today we realize that our neighbor is our self." A half hour later, I learned that my friend and colleague, Cantor Susan Wehle, was on that plane; and never in my life did those words from scripture hang so heavy on my heart. Susan and I worked with Othman Shibley, from the Islamic Center, on the interfaith youth event last spring. We had lunch together many times, and this spring I was planning to address her students at the Jewish high school where she taught on Lutherans and other Christians. Susan was an inspiration to me, and she was extremely grounded in her faith. On Friday night, Jerilyn and I attended the "Shabbat" worship at Temple Beth Am, and told many of her parishioners how we were touched by her presence and inspired by her faith. For me, Susan will always be a voice of "healing and hope."

Which was the title of a CD I purchased from Susan a couple of years ago, after another interfaith event at the Temple. I would like you to hear her voice. This first piece is called: *B'ruchot HaBa-ot.* The words say: "May you be blessed beneath the wings of Shechinah" (a grammatically feminine word that means the *dwelling* or *settling,* and it is used to describe the dwelling presence of God, either in the Temple or in your heart): "Be blessed with love; Be blessed with peace."

Susan will always be a voice of "healing and hope."

In the Gospel lesson this morning, a leper approached Jesus, and kneeled before him and begged for help. The rest of the world viewed the leper as unclean, and unfit to be out in public, but this unclean leper (this person outside the norm of society) came to Jesus and begged: "If you choose, you have the power to make me clean." Jesus stretched out his hand and touched him, and said to him, "I do choose. Be made clean." Immediately the disease of leprosy left the man and he was healed.

Jesus had a very powerful touch—the power to heal and comfort. Jesus' touch caused miracles to happen. We may not be able to cause miracles to happen as Jesus did, but each one of us is given the opportunity to use God's love to touch others in ways that comfort and heal.

Susan Wehle had that healing touch. When I was in the hospital a few years ago with my cellulites episode, a number of people came to visit me, including Pastor Charlie Greene (who welcomed me as a colleague when I first came to WNY 12 years ago), Pastor John Scarifia (the dean of our conference) and my good friend, Pastor Tim Madsen. They all prayed with me, and they all prayed for my healing; but when Susan came to visit, she sang to the glory of God for my healing. Another song on her CD is called "The Healing Circle." The words go like this:

Life is a circle, love is the song,

Peace is the story we've yearned for so long.

When we surrender to God in all things,

The circle is completed,

Our hearts are blessed with wings.

In my mind, and in my heart, Susan will always be God's voice of "healing and hope."

But it can never stop there. Jesus had the power to heal simply by touching the leper; Susan had the power to heal because God had blessed her with a beautiful voice and an unwavering faith; you and I have been given opportunities to be healing and hope in an unclean world; you and I have gifts to share, and stories to tell; we have the power to heal and comfort, and while we may not be able to cause miracles like Jesus, we certainly can wrap ourselves around our neighbor, and try to love our neighbor as we love ourselves, because today I know that my neighbor is my self.

This last song from Susan is called the "Circle Chant," and it repeats four times, so if you want to join your voice with Susan's voice the words are very simple:

"Circle round for freedom, circle round for peace,

For all of us imprisoned, circle for release.

Circle for the planet, circle for each soul;

For the children of our children, keep the circle whole."

AMEN.

"Susan's Piano" by Karen Chernick

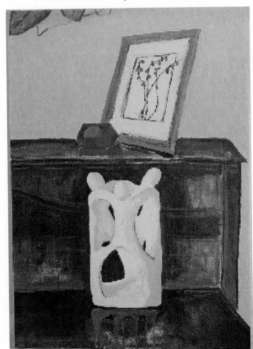

Vignette

Laura Masters

"This salad just makes me feel so righteous." Susan said this while chopping the kale.

"Yea, I know what you mean, kale is just so strong. It would have been better if Popeye ate kale than spinach," her sister, Dana, responded in her honest Brooklyn accent.

"I agree, spinach with its wilty leaves, but kale retains its structure even when soaked in water for a while," Susan replied.

Together they prepared the salad. Kale, lemon, olive oil, walnuts, cucumbers and tomatoes. They cracked the walnuts in another room because Jacob's girlfriend had an allergy.

"Ob la di, ob la da, life goes on, rah! Lalala life goes on." Susan sang while they cooked, along to the White Album by the Beatles. Next was "Wild Honey Pie." She danced in the kitchen and belted the words out with the full capacity of her diaphragm.

"Honey pie, honey pie," Jacob sang along while staring at his girlfriend.

"I don't think I've ever heard that song before," Susan told him while "Bungalow Bill" played loudly.

The lasagna was almost done. In the oven, bubbling with ricotta and cheddar and mozzarella, "not the way the Italians do it," she apologized to the girlfriend because she's Italian, "but still good."

Everyone agreed that it was good and while they ate The Beatles came off and Chopin went on for more egregious digestion. Later they played Boggle and Dana asked what else there was, if there was anything to drink besides the Riesling and water they had had with dinner. Susan told her no, there was some soymilk, but that was it. If she wanted, Dana could find some Clementines in the fridge. Dana grabbed three, one for Susan, one for Jacob and his girlfriend to share and one for herself. They pulled white strings of rind off the Clementines and Jacob showed his trick of peeling the skin off in a spiral. Triumphantly with a bit of smug, he spiraled it back in the form of a Clementine and handed it to his girlfriend to his right, she laughed and told him she didn't want it. Feigning hurt, he turned away, got up, and threw out everyone's rinds. Dana goaded Sue into making a face, the face that she made as a younger mom to get the boys to laugh, her boys. It's the same face Jacob makes now to make the girlfriend laugh. It always works, never fails. Everyone wiped tears from the corners of their eyes in the midst of the laughter after she made the face.

Later in the evening Jacob and his girlfriend went to watch a movie and Dana and Sue sat in the living room. Talking and laughing, they sat and were with each other.

Three months later it would not happen again. That would be the last dinner, the last chance, the last of everything was in that night. The last hug.

"Ob la di, ob la da, life goes on, ra! La la la la life goes on."

Some Reflections on *MaYakar Chasdecha* During Mourning

Maggid Andrew Gold

The early stages of the mourning process, perhaps akin to the Sheloshim period, are filled with potential, perhaps even pregnant with the possibility of new birth—if we're willing to venture through that temporary crack in the doorway between worlds. As one's loved one has departed from this life, the mourner's world has been torn asunder. While this feels excruciatingly painful, that pain must be engaged and honored. As we do so, the ground of one's being is tilled, turned inside out, and rests achingly fertile.

Old assumptions about everything—Life, Death, God, Goodness, Compassion, Justness, Order, Chaos, Purpose, Plan, and 'who' it is that grieves — are all cast into the tumultuousness of Not Knowing. Not Knowing in the best and most sacred sense. In the sense that awe, in the moment of recognizing the undeniable hand of Unknowable Mystery, takes the breath away... allows for an empty space into which, when the time is right, may rush the gift of guidance, the sweet kiss of the breath of life renewed and transformed.

Ultimately the assumptions of knowing that underlie each of our 'personal stories', the constructs that seek to substantiate our understandings of this world, must eventually be uprooted lest we wither. Yet few of us are at all eager to enter into those particular depths that lay bare the root of our soul.

Enter unfathomable Death!

And so as I have begun to move through my anger with God, having spoken at some length and in relatively un-edited terms lifnei Yah, in the face of the Holy One, I find myself once more drawn under my Tallit. Hesitantly, I open my lips (wanting after all, to be true to my sense of outrage...) and declare Ma yakar chasdecha Elohim, "How precious is Your loving-kindness, oh God."

The Tallit that forms my mishkan, that sometimes are the arms of a loving parent, sometimes the wings of Shekhinah, and sometimes the bed sheets of intimacy with the Beloved, and eventually will be the shroud that I too will be buried in, today, finally, becomes the filaments of a chrysalis that gently holds me as I wait and allow myself to be re-ensouled.

Author's notes for clarification:

The prayer Ma yakar chasdecha Elohim (How precious is Your loving-kindness, oh God) is a traditional part of the Jewish morning prayer liturgy. It is said while donning the Tallit, the prayer shawl which is used for daily prayer, and is often used as the marriage canopy during one's wedding, and is also commonly used as one's burial shroud. The tallit, used throughout one's life, thus becomes a very intimate spiritual garment in accessing communion with the Divine. As such it can become a 'personal mishkan', the portable tabernacle where God's presence, Shekhinah, dwells and welcomes.

This particular prayer, of acknowledging the preciousness of God's loving kindness in one's life, has been a central part of my personal daily practice for many years. In the days and weeks following Susan's death, I was unable to utter these words. After about a month, known as the sheloshim period (the 30 days after a death), haltingly, and with great struggle, I began to be able to reclaim the prayer for myself.

Farewell, My Friend

Sheldon Soman

In memory of Cantor Susan Wehle

When I first heard the news
I couldn't believe it
It must be a mistake
It just couldn't be true
We couldn't have lost you
Who brought so much life
      into our world.
Who brought a song into our hearts
Who brought a smile into our lives
      and brightened our days.
How could G-d take you from us?
How could your candle burn out?

Time has passed
I am left with so many questions
      but no answers.
My tears will dry
The scars will heal
When I think of you, the pain will always be there.
      The tears will fall yet again
But your smile will never fade,
Your light will always shine.

Reason
Carrie Gardner

A guy I used to date works at the Clarence Center Coffee House
pretty close to where it happened.
He had thick, rolling blonde hair and a face like a kid
rosy and peachy and fair; smooth and kind.
There's always one in the crowd. Women flock to boys like this—
devilishly beautiful albeit inconsequential on the grand scale of love.
There had to be at least one of them on that plane.
When we heard about the crash, we were driving home from Alden
waiting at the light at the corner of Brighton and Colvin, anxious
to get home, turn on the television and dress for bed.
We just wanted to be safe and warm and private, since no one
cared about us that night.
Everyone cared about the passengers.
When my husband and I looked at each other, we feared the worse
but ached and prayed anyway. We thought about parents and
sons and daughters and friends, content or tortured
hopeful or resigned.

We want to believe that everything happens for a reason
but remain unclear, murky, suspicious.
Plain exposure doesn't seem enough;
seems the kind of event that
makes us question the fiber of our souls—
an urge to doubt in the face of what causes us
to be faithful.

Yoga Class

Laura Masters

I had forgotten that it was the 12th, that it was also Thursday the 12th—the day down to the day of the week of a six-month anniversary that no one would ever want. I had decided to go to yoga at the same studio as Susan, the one that I had been to only when she was there or only when I was with her son, my boyfriend. Today would be my first class alone, without either of them.

The first time we went, it was all three of us. In the car before class she told us about her secret competition with the teacher—so secret, that even he didn't know. At the end or beginning of class there is a breath meditation on "Ohm" for one full breath, and she tried to hold hers longer than the instructor held his. I listened at the end of that class, after my own breath had ended—as had her son's next to me—and everyone else fell out. Meanwhile one male and one female voice still rang, resonating like water around a bowl. Just as slowly as it started, the instructor's breath ended and there was one ringing voice left, Susan's. It sounded as true and clear as a pebble dropped in water to create concentric circles.

The class on my own was liberating. I felt as if I really could do it by myself, even if she had gone there, even if we had gone only together, even if she wouldn't be there. We all lay down at the end of class to relax and meditate. There was a small rumbling in my diaphragm, and it traveled slowly up my throat to my sinuses where water began to collect in the corners of my eyes. I didn't understand this emotion; I had thought I was fine, that I could handle this and just kept breathing. My hands were out at my sides, my palms turned up. Something pushed into my left palm, heavy like a glass paperweight but soft like fleece. I didn't dare open my eyes. I just breathed through this profound moment and concentrated on the breath, cool as it hit the back of my throat and warm as it exited my nostrils. Her presence hovered in the room, infused the air we all breathed together.

"Everyone turn to your right side and slowly, gently, push yourself up with your arms to sitting position." We all did as instructed, no one rebelled to remain horizontal and fall asleep. "Now, breathe one deep breath in and we'll let it all out as one Ohm."

My breath filled my entire cavity; my diaphragm expanded and my voice rounded out of my mouth, creating the letter O until I could no longer hold it, then humming an M. The woman behind me, Jean, with her long dark hair and olive skin, her son sitting next to her on a mat, had just joined the class about ten minutes. She began her "Ohm" in a voice pure and honest. As each Ohm dropped out of the group, there were two voices left, one male and one female. And as the instructor's voice—lower than the female's—fell to silent, we all heard what I thought I would never again hear, a thick, syrupy female voice ringing at the end on "mmmm" standing alone.

Thank you, Susan. Thank you, Jean.

Toward the Light

(Flight 3407, Clarence Center, NY)

Jane Sadowsky

When eagles fall from the sky
and houses crack open like eggs,
the world, too far, too fast, too full,
stills.

A beacon of distress.
We turn from our daily lives.
We turn as one.

In that instant when the soul releases,
climbs the night's smoke to the heavens,
earthly hearts contract.
All that we knew, iced over now, shatters.

Sirens lace the night air.
Loved ones blown free from the wreckage,
climb also, toward the light.
In the heart of a neighborhood, impossible flame blooms.

In the silence beyond hearing, music.
Mournful saxophone, gentle guitar,
sweet female voice rising in prayer.
Notes ascend, escorting our neighbors

home.

Cantor Susan Wehle: A 'Spiritual Sister' of Anne Frank[1]

Barbara D. Miller

We can never know Anne Frank as a woman in her prime, but can see and benefit from her ideals, alive as they are in others. One true 'soul sister' of Anne is Cantor Susan Wehle of Temple Beth Am, Williamsville, whose exquisite voice was stilled when flight 3407 went down over Clarence. Though lost not as a young girl, but as a mature community leader at what ought to have been the mid point in a highly giving and productive life, Susan had in common with Anne an intense vitality. Like Anne, she lived the years she was granted in joy, originality and generosity. To borrow a phrase from Buffalo State College's "Anne Frank Project," Susan Wehle might be the model for the "artist as peacemaker," especially through her interfaith and youth outreach.

The original essay from which this article derives also addressed the long life and contributions of Dr. Fanni Bogdanow, who endured the horrors of *Kristallnacht* and whose parents survived Auschwitz and Bergen Belsen. Dr. Bogdanow, a member of Anne Frank's generation, was thus honored together with Cantor Wehle at the first annual Anne Frank conference on September 11th, 2009. Renowned world wide among scholars of Arthurian literature,[2] Dr. Bogdanow is Professor Emeritus of the University of Manchester, England. Having settled in the greater Manchester region after being taken in by an English family through the famous *Kindertransport*, she thus embodies the conference theme, "Survival and the Power of Testimony."

It should be also be noted by way of introduction that my Anne Frank Project presentation was significantly enriched by the readings and musical selections of poet and classical guitarist, Temple Beth Am's Dr. Gunilla Theander Kester (coeditor of this anthology), to whom I am most grateful. The presentation's overarching message was that all three women's lives considered through it can and should inspire the best in us, and that we should never underestimate the connections binding us as members of the human race.

When I first proposed to take part in the Buffalo State conference, a colleague asked me what Anne Frank could possibly have to do with my field of study. Her obvious implication was that my professional work ought not to stray too far outside the traditional parameters of my degree discipline, which is the language and literature of Spain. But as someone whose research has highlighted the border-crossings of Arthurian literature from England to France and from both these countries to Spain, it has never seemed prudent, or even possible, to be limited by such imaginary (and unstable) lines as geopolitical frontiers or the arbitrary impositions dividing study fields. And so I told my doubtful colleague that the surprising ways, means and effects of interdisciplinary and intercommunity crossroads experienced in my individual professional life, had been merged into the point of departure for this ultimately biographical offering whose primary subject (in this iteration) is Cantor Susan Wehle. Moreover, as Cantor Wehle herself might have pointed out, the nature of the path that led me to her provides a very important prelude before full engagement in the topic. This is because of the pervading motif of junctures between and among us, which forms at least an implicit aspect of any biography, and certainly stands as a touchstone of hers.

Ever since experiencing the reactions of my students during a class I was teaching in 2001, entitled "Civilizations and Cultures of Spain," I have been studying everything I can about the coexistence on the Iberian Peninsula of Jews, Christians and Moslems (a defining element of the culture of medieval Spain), and also about the religions as such, both outside, and inside, Iberia. All engaged college and university faculty members pursue their own brands of professional development. In my case related to the issues I am mentioning here, a kind of professional and personal mandate rushed in with irresistible force after September

11th of my first year on the Buffalo State faculty, when my shocked and uncomprehending students asked such questions as how their textbooks could present Spanish Arab culture as exceptionally accomplished and humane, when Middle Eastern terrorists who called themselves practicing Moslems had just killed some of those they knew and loved, along with thousands of other innocent people.

The answers, of course, are intensely complex. Therefore what struck me was that I had to pursue a deeper understanding of the three monotheisms, even though this is a topic I have always found interesting and that was involved in one of my published articles years before coming to Buffalo State. But now I felt something beyond even a passionate interest in the subject. Now I knew that I had to grasp it better than ever before, that I owed it to my students and that I simply could not fail them in this. So for instance I have attended Rabbi Isaac Klein Scholar-in-Residence weekends and participated in Bible study sessions and Jewish film nights at Temple Shaarey Zedek (now Temple Beth Tzedek) in Amherst, and have been reading the Hebrew Bible page by page, with the plan to progress to the Christian New Testament and the Moslem Koran. I have always believed in going to the source of things.[3]

All this eventually led me and a group of my students to a unique Western New York interfaith and University-at-Buffalo-sponsored conference held in November of 2004 entitled "A Golden Age in Spain: The Convivencia of Jews, Christians and Moslems in Medieval Spain."[4] One element of this four-day, magnificently orchestrated series of meetings, lectures and exhibits was an open Sabbath service at Temple Beth Am, Williamsville, to which all participants were invited. On the Friday evening of the event, eminent scholar of African Studies Dr. Sulayman Nyang of Howard University, who happens to be a practicing Moslem, spoke to an integrated congregation from a Jewish pulpit, about opening a dialogue together and opening our hearts to one another, to make our connections more deliberate, positive and purposeful.

That night was my first encounter with the beauty of a Jewish worship service, and the joyous and welcoming atmosphere inherent to it. Representing all this to a great extent was a very remarkable woman by the name of Cantor Susan Wehle, whose smile lit up the entire sanctuary. When Cantor Wehle offered the gift of her gorgeous voice, and lifted her arms to lead responses during the service, I had the distinct impression as if she were actually opening her arms to embrace everyone there. One had only to see her, especially in that setting, to know real inspiration. And it is my particular aim in this essay to tell you more about this woman, who reached out to comfort others, to heal them and to teach them, by following her own uniquely creative and loving path.

One lesson that has become clearer to me by studying the life of Anne Frank, and those of the impressive women who I think of as her spiritual sisters, is to concentrate on the good of constructive attitude and action. And while people may often kindly say "God bless," the miracle is that we can be the instruments of blessing, and even *become* the blessings ourselves. Anne Frank once wrote, "Think of all the beauty that's still left in and around you and be happy." An enduring example of such beauty indeed is the voice and spirit of Cantor Susan Wehle. And we are blessed that a recording of that eloquent voice remains to aid our contemplations and to fire our better natures. Even more, we are blessed that such soaring spirits as hers are deathless.

As alluded to above, the original presentation of which this essay's basis formed a part addressed two women born at the cusp of the 1930s, Fanni Bogdanow and Anne Frank, one who is the eternal girl, the other, the distinguished and senior erudite. From that standpoint we were able to complete by contrast a kind of generational triangle through the story of Susan Wehle, who at the end of her earthly life was neither a young girl like Anne, nor a venerable scholar like Fanni. Susan Wehle, born in the 1950s in the United States, was in the full flowering of life, a mother of two young adult sons, a leader in the Jewish community, and a tireless participant in many initiatives for the greater community of Western New York and beyond.

Since it was so appropriate to name Cantor Wehle and to honor her at the 2009 Anne Frank conference, in part because her loss was still so fresh, it seemed only right as well briefly to reflect upon the lives of others who had died with her. It was not practical to name all fifty of the lost through flight 3407 in that context. But at least we noted that all were precious to their friends and families, that all were valuable human beings, and even that many of them were very uncommon contributors. As a way of memorializing them all implicitly, we named four in addition to Cantor Wehle who were a part of the Buffalo State community, or who in some way seemed especially to reflect the spirit of the presentation, as follows:

Alison Des Forges, of Buffalo, was senior advisor for Human Rights Watch's Africa division, and one of the world's leading experts on the genocide in Rawanda. She testified at eleven trials at the International Criminal Tribunal for Rawanda as such.

Beverly Eckert, a Buffalo State alumna, was a 9/11 widow whose husband, Sean Rooney, died in the World Trade Center attacks. Beverly would not have been on that plane to Buffalo in February, 2009 if it hadn't been for an annual presentation of a scholarship award begun in 2002, planned for the following day at Canisius High School, in honor of her beloved Sean. She had been generous to Canisius in this context because of her conviction that education should be supported in order to make a difference. Beverly was also headed to Buffalo in order to celebrate Sean's memory on his birthday, February 15th, with members of his family and with friends, all of whom happen to be Buff State graduates.

Maddy Loftus, a recent Buffalo State graduate, was headed to Buffalo for a weekend reunion of Bengals women hockey players. Maddy was a star of the team, for instance scoring three goals during one weekend in 2003, and being honored as Buffalo State athlete of the week for that stellar performance.

One more young woman who was lost on February 12th, 2009 was Mary Julia Abraham, a retired Army Reserve First Sergeant and a Greyhound rescuer. A Licensed Practical Nurse and a Respiratory Therapist as well, Mary had spent that last day, three days after her fortieth-fourth birthday, teaching a disabled veteran how to operate and care for his electric wheelchair. Though Mary had no direct connection to Buffalo State, I thanked those present at the Anne Frank conference for allowing me to name her, because she was a member of my own extended family, being my husband Richard's second cousin.

Given the untried nature of the Anne Frank event at the time it was first announced, I was unsure whether others would agree that a fitting presentation could involve intersections between Western New York and world events such as 9/11 and the February, 2009 plane crash, integrated with the ethnic and religious concerns that were clearly central to the conference, yet addressing all this through the somewhat unusual approach of biographical portraits and personal observations. So I sketched out the preliminary concept that would form the basis of my proposal in an e-mail to conference organizer Professor Drew Kahn. He responded in part "I knew Cantor Wehle and believe it would be a well deserved tribute to her and the Jewish community to "sing" her memories. . . She is deeply missed."

Thus encouraged, I devised an overview of Cantor Wehle's biography, based on articles from *The Buffalo News*, the Temple Beth Am, Williamsville web site, and other published materials, beginning with the fact of her sixteen-year leadership within the Buffalo Jewish community. Most sources further highlight that receiving her Cantorial Smicha (ordination) from Aleph, the Movement for Jewish Renewal, she was Cantor at Temple Beth Am from 2002 until her death, and was previously a cantorial soloist at Amherst's Temple Sinai for nine years. Cantor Wehle was also a life member of Hadassah, and a member of the American Conference of Cantors. Though naturally all this impressed me, I had yet to learn that in addition to her University at Buffalo degree in Judaic studies, Susan Wehle completed a degree program in theater, and another in acting from the Goodman School of Drama. Integrating these accomplishments and putting them to creatively constructive use involved her appearances with theater companies in Buffalo, Chicago and New York. And this formed a perfect background for her teaching of musical and spiritual workshops, as well as her conducting of youth and adult choirs.

Beyond the importance of finding and recording the facts of all the achievements and activities just cited, it had actually become clear to me before knowing about the Anne Frank Project, by attending her memorial service, that Susan Wehle's family was extraordinarily close, and that even in light of her more obvious accomplishments, rich endeavors, and dearly held friends, being the mother of her sons Jonah and Jacob was for her the unrivaled and crowning jewel of her life.

The salient point for the context at hand, however, is more general. The broader portrait I had begun to perceive by talking with those who knew Cantor Wehle well depicted an unusually busy and successful woman, whose driving passion was the love of God and of others, and who channelled these primal and religious forces into an exceptional life of service. In fact, what I found most specifically inspirational while piecing together her story, was the synergistic fulfillment of her devout and community-motivated purpose, because she had managed it so directly through her individual talents. A clear example of this synergy relates to her rendering (accompanied on guitar by Gunilla Kester) of Debbie Friedman's irresistibly beautiful song, "L'chi Lach," with its telling refrain "you shall be a blessing," which it was possible to play for the Buffalo State-Anne

Frank audience, via the compact disk entitled "Songs of Healing and Hope." It needs to be underscored that considering the life of the vocalist, this title is not just a nice sounding phrase, appropriate to a faith-based setting, for Cantor Wehle lived in accord with it by using music, as a direct and active instrument of healing.

It should be clarified that as I am using the term here, a "healing" is not necessarily synonymous with a cure. Though it can be searingly difficult to accept, sometimes a person's only possible release from suffering is through death. Cantor Susan Wehle sang at the bedsides of many who were sick, in recovery, or dying. According to anecdotes I've been privileged to hear, in more than one case Susan stayed and sang to a person even in his or her last moments. Perhaps for some their final perception in this world was of that elegantly devout and gallantly reassuring voice.

It is striking that even the brilliant form of giving just related made but a single facet of a life like a jewel. For instance we might consider Cantor Wehle's work with interfaith groups, in pursuit of bringing us closer to world peace. As her friend the Reverend Gail Lewis has expressed it, "Susan was a bridge-builder."[5] Cantor Wehle also championed women's causes, even apart from showing through her own life what a woman can achieve. In fact she could occasionally become feisty about gender-equality issues, as happened in the course of her liturgical debates and discussions with her Rabbi, Irwin Tanenbaum. Most of all though, there was always, in every aspect from music to interfaith projects, the nurturance, acceptance and encouragement of children. Not only did she teach children to sing, and to become ready for Bar and Bat Mitzvahs. She brought together young people from the Islamic, Christian and Jewish communities, showing them how to reach out to one another, to respect and learn from their differences, and to become friends who could enrich one another's lives by understanding how much they had in common.[6] One particular that appeals to me from my stance as a language professor is Cantor

Wehle's participation in vacation Bible schools for Christian children where she taught Jewish songs and led some very young Western New Yorkers in dance, even gently correcting the Hebrew spellings found in their books, produced by Christian publishers, "so that we could actually say what we meant to say."

One of the songs that Susan sang is entitled "Circle Chant," and contains the memorable lines ". . .Circle for the planet, circle for each soul, for the children of our children, keep the circle whole." To begin closing the circle formed here, I'd like to return emphatically to the subject of Cantor Wehle's enormous energy. Temple Beth Am Executive Assistant N. Jo Tufts, one of her best and most beloved friends, told me that in this world where none of us ever seems to have enough time, Susan practically manufactured it. Her calendar might be jammed on any given day. But if she happened to hear that someone was in the hospital she would have one arm in her coat as she grabbed her keys and checked which hospital and room while passing the temple secretary's desk on her way out the door. She would go straight for a visit, including some singing, and be back in about an hour, never breaking stride as she continued on with the rest of that day. It made me tired just to think of it, all the while it stirred me to wonder if I shouldn't try such an approach myself (or whether it might be wise to refrain from too literal an imitation of such a super woman).

I could have written a great deal more based on remarks from Cantor Wehle's memorial service, and on conversations with her family and friends.[i] But the main points for the themes we celebrated in the context of the Anne Frank project, as they played out in her life, have already been highlighted. So I offer as a summarizing idea that contrast between urgency and importance made famous by Dr. Stephen Covey. As he has told us in his perennial *The Seven Habits of Highly Effective People*, that which is urgent is not always important, in the sense of lasting significance. Cantor Wehle knew the difference, and acted in wise harmony with that understanding. In fact the better I have "gotten to know her" in the only way I could, through these conversations with those close to her, the more I realize how much there is to learn from her. Like Anne Frank and like Fanni Bogdanow, Susan Wehle will always be here in a way, always teaching, always singing, always creating time by moving others to be their best selves as humane achievers, if we are open to her presence, and to the presence of the sacred that was and is so much part of her, and that can be found if we will only take on the habit of looking for the best in each other.

Finally, a theme shown in all the lives we considered at the conference is the will to face and endure evils, but never to be governed by bitterness or hatred in return. Both of Susan Wehle's parents survived the horrors of Auschwitz. Yet her entire life was about compassion, joy and healing so that as with the other two women honored in the original presentation, we encounter the resiliency of a life shadowed by the horrors of the Shoah, and yet whose light utterly transcends it.

At the memorial service for Cantor Wehle, a young woman (as it happens the daughter of Gunilla Kester), spoke to the congregation. This young woman, whose lyrical name is Shiri Sophia Kester (Shiri being the Hebrew word for "song") is deeply involved in the youth activities of her congregation, and spoke about how hard it would be to go on without her beloved Cantor, this astonishing role model whom she and her friends had loved so much. The most important thing Shiri said, was that she and her friends must go on because that is what Susan herself would want. This is, of course, essentially the kind of sentiment for which the diary of Anne Frank has always been known. As Susan Wehle might have appreciated, on September 11th, 2009 we had considered her life among those of three special women, two writers, one singer, juxtaposed as a trio of metaphorical sisters. And though each of them is wondrously unique, the combined and interconnected message they bring us is all one: that the stories and the songs go on as we carry them forward, as we make them ours, and as we offer them to each other.

[1] This essay derives from a section of a more extensive presentation entitled "Sisters of Anne Frank: Three Women, One Legacy." The original talk was given during Buffalo State College's first annual Anne Frank Project, which took place on September 11th, 2009. More information about this ongoing and evolving human-rights awareness endeavor is available at www.theannefrankproject.com. For more about Buffalo State, which recently assumed full ownership of this project based in the Theater Department under the leadership of Department Chair, Professor Drew Kahn, please refer to www.buffalostate.edu.

[2] Arthurian literature is literature relating to, or inspired by, the legends of King Arthur.

[3] Many thanks are due Rabbi A. Charles Shalman, formerly of Temple Shaarey Zedek, for his friendship and his ongoing patient dialogue with me about Judaism. I first met Rabbi Shalman, a student of early-Sephardic poetry expert Dr. Raymond P. Scheindlin, at the Network of Western New York Religious Communities conference on Spain. And it was Rabbi Shalman who afforded me the opportunity to participate in numerous study-related activities at his synagogue. I would also like to acknowledge the members of his congregation, who welcomed me with unfailing warmth and kindness.

[4] For information on the organization which spearheaded the Convivencia-in-Spain conference, the Western New York Network of Religious Communities, see www.religiousnet.org.

[5] As Cantor Wehle herself might have viewed it, the quotations montage read by students from my Fall, 2009 "Survey of Spanish Literature" class, not only capped the original presentation in the literal sense of providing its last words, but added a truly outstanding feature, superlatively carried out. The students' names are Adam Kibat, Hilary Leninger, Tabitha Torres, Brittany Vandermeulen and Sonia Veiga.

[6] Another connection, in the sense of striking coincidences and parallels, is that Beverly Eckert, mentioned above, was honored posthumously, on September 10, 2009 during the annual 9/11 commemorative events, with the "Building Bridges" award, by the organization "Voices of September 11." I am grateful to Beverly's sister, Karen Eckert for sharing this and other impressive details for inclusion in this article.

[7] I would like to acknowledge all those I've been privileged to meet during the research for this article, particularly Temple Beth Am Executive Assistant N. Jo Tufts, Rev. Gail Lewis (who is, in effect, an auxiliary member of Temple Beth Am), and Rabbi Irwin Tanenbaum, who made themselves available without limit for interviews and other intensive conversations. Perhaps most of all my husband Richard and I have cherished the chance to meet Susan's sisters, Eva Friedner and Dana Wehle. And this was made possible through the love and commitment of Gunilla and Daniel Kester, who have encircled us as if we had always belonged in their midst. The openness of all these new friends in sharing their insights and memories has been remarkable considering the shattering nature of their own grief. So I wish to say that my gratitude is boundless, much like their warmth, generosity and patience. In thinking of Anne Frank's observation on beauty, even in the midst of pain, I can only reply that such new friendships as those generated through this project must be what Anne had in mind, and that I hope the publishable version of this article can convey some measure of what the opportunity to stand with them has meant to me.

"Going to the First Saved Message...."
Edward G. Wright

Please enter your password, then press pound
You have no new messages
And
You have one saved voice message
To listen to your message press one

First saved voice message:

"Hi babe, it's me, just boarding now.
See you when I get there. Can't wait."

End of messages
There are no more messages
To erase this message press seven
To hear this message again press one

Going to the first saved message

"Hi babe, it's me . . ."

And again and again . . .

Excerpts From a D'var Torah in Memory of Cantor Susan Wehle

Judy Henn

(Presented at a Shabbaton in Ancaster, Ontario, June 13, 2009)

I've been asked to give this D'var Torah in Susan's memory, to somehow bring a sense of her into this beautiful Shabbat morning. Susan would often begin our Friday night Erev Shabbat service with a *niggun*, a wordless melody. She always took pains to explain that, when you sing a *niggun*, it's not because you can't remember the words. It's because the feelings you are trying to express are so powerful that words are inadequate. Well, when I think about Susan Wehle, words are inadequate...but I'll do my best.

Susan loved the natural beauty of God's world. It was one of the things which drew her to this beautiful setting year after year. She felt refreshed, renewed, energized and peaceful. Just as Judaism emerged from the Jewish people's experience in the desert, so Susan was shaped by all things in nature, from a mountaintop in New Mexico to the woods of Ontario, to the flower boxes she lovingly planted every spring.

If you ask 20 people what was the most outstanding quality that Susan Wehle possessed, 19 of them would say, "Her spirituality." I'd be one of those 19, but her spirituality was grounded in a love and concern for all people here on earth. Out of the depths of her very Jewish soul, she truly believed that, only through interfaith outreach, could we ensure the continuation of a viable community. I knew that her activities extended beyond Temple Beth Am but, until this tragic plane crash brought so many people together to honor her life, I had no idea how far-reaching her influence really was.

So who was Susan Wehle? Words are inadequate. She was a cantor, a teacher, a counselor, a mother, a sister, a friend. She was funny and serious, outgoing and contemplative. She once told me that she was so happy that she found her calling, her passion, her purpose. I'm happy that, after 13 years of hard work, while also working full-time and raising two boys as a single mom, she was able to attain her Cantorial S'micha through Aleph, the Jewish Renewal movement. I can't say it any better than her dear friend, Maggid Andy Gold, speaking at her memorial service in February. He said "Cantors are taught to sing from the diaphragm. Susan sang from the heart."

May her memory be for a blessing.

Conjugating Grief

Gunilla Theander Kester

(For Susan)

Promised Land. Should I ever find
you on my own, turn me to salt
if you wish, but I will step
over your threshold backward.

When you meet your Moses, taking you
through the desert to the promised land,
do you always know it? Do you know
you must arrive alone?

Past tense: Hallelujah, I get it. I am fluent in
Egypt, slavery, hard labor and bitter herbs.

Future tense—@ present scrambled. Can't de-
cipher its hieroglyphics, useless text.

Yet that conditional tense, effort of
every moment, my constant companion:

> *What if?*
> *What if?*
> *If only?*

Clarence Finds Ways to Ease the Pain

Michelle Kearns, Buffalo News Staff Reporter

Buffalo News, March 07, 2009

David Gardner's sad, surreal experience with the crash of Continental Flight 3407, and his desire to find a way to help, began when he went to his sunroom to see what his dogs were barking about.

He saw flames out the window and turned on the TV. He then kept looking from one to the other. From the window to the TV and back again.

"I don't know what to say. I don't know what to do," he remembered thinking. "It was a numbing experience."

A few days later he got an idea, and designed a fund-raising T-shirt of a broken heart with a Band-Aid. "I guess it's helping me heal," he said.

This is a sentiment shared by others in a community looking for a way to transform its sorrow into something constructive. The tragedy that claimed 50 lives has led to a series of projects, some in the works, some unfolding now: From the heart T-shirts to commemorative light-pole banners to raising money for a town clock with a plaque for crash victims.

"It's whatever people want to do that helps them feel a little better, that helps them heal," said Lori Adams, a volunteer coordinator, who was selling the T-shirts at Eastern Hills Mall Friday afternoon. "It's not just T-shirts. We're trying to coordinate any effort."

Other projects on Adams' list include arrangements under way at the Clarence Center fire hall for a commemorative June race and concert. There are more plans for more concerts.

A group of Clarence mothers made thank-you notes that are now being handwritten to all the people in the emergency crews and first responders.

Volunteers have made plans to take down the ribbons on trees and telephone poles when they get too battered. Local florists donated them in black, for sorrow, and white, for hope.

Mark Woodward, the town historian, also has begun to set up a series of days for videotaping and recording people's stories before sharp memories of the experience fade.

Adams, a real estate broker and convenience store owner, started to pitch in after sending an e-mail offer of help to the town. This led to the job of volunteer coordinator at the ad-hoc command center in Town Hall.

Throughout the 11-day cleanup after the crash, Adams was moved, sometimes to tears, by all the people who came to help: One boy arrived every day with a basket of cookies for volunteers. So many restaurants offered food to the emergency crews that she had to schedule a rotation so there wouldn't be an overabundance. One day an elderly woman brought in a new purse she'd filled with everything a woman might need to give to Karen Wielinski, whose husband died when the plane crashed on their house.

"Everybody has their own little piece to give," Adams said.

For Debbie Lesinski, it was upsetting to have to leave Clarence the morning after the crash, when she wanted to stay and help. Instead, the interior decorator had to attend the Hamburg home and garden show, where she had a booth.

A few evenings later, she organized a meeting in her kitchen with other local women. They decided to sell new commemorative banners for town light poles.

For $225 or less, people can help sponsor a banner that says, "Tomorrow . . . Together & Stronger." Money raised will help pay for a town street clock in tribute to last year's bicentennial, as originally planned in part by the Clarence Center Community Association.

But now, banner money also will help pay for a plaque for crash victims that will be affixed to the clock.

"There is a driving need to help," said Lesinski. "I was gone for the weekend, and I felt like I wasn't here to do my share."

Lesinski and Adams also were pitching in at the T-shirt selling table at Eastern Hills Mall, where there will be one final day of sales from 10 a.m. to 4 p.m. today.

Clarence's New Buffalo Shirt Factory, where the shirts were made by workers who donated their time, will donate the proceeds. Sales were expected to raise about $30,000 for a Flight 3407 fund, managed by the Community Foundation, to help people whose lives were affected by the crash.

Gardner, who is known for inventing a technique for printing bright designs on black T-shirts — a favorite of such clients as Harley-Davidson and the Rolling Stones — said the heart shirt seems to be helping in another way, too.

He found a way to make the Band-Aid look three-dimensional. He's been noticing that the effect makes people immediately try to feel the fabric and see if the bandage is real. The move to touch the shirt then sparks conversation. People often end up talking about someone they cared about who died.

"I think it gives people maybe a jumping-off point. It's hard to even broach the subject," he said. "I think that's the only way you do heal . . . You find that sharing it with other people is a way to come to peace with it yourself."

Reprinted by permission of the author and The Buffalo News.

Alison's Book

Rachel Fix Dominguez

The following memories of Alison Des Forges were compiled by Rachel Fix Dominguez. Most of the contributors were connected to Alison through her work at Bennett Park Montessori Center (PS#32) in Buffalo. Alison was one of the founding parents of the school. As a former student of BPMC, friend of the family, and admirer of Alison's tireless quest for social justice in ways large and small, Rachel felt it important to collect memories of Alison's work on behalf of children. These memories are also being compiled into book form for Alison's three grandchildren, so that they have a record of the many ways in which their grandmother helped to improve educational opportunities in Buffalo.

I apologize that the first memory to come into my head about Alison is so very specific. I remember that, back in the early '80s, she usually kept Brown Cow yogurt in their fridge. Not jam-bottomed Dannon or silky Yoplait, but lumpy, sour, plain Brown Cow.

I can remember nowhere else I'd rather play than with Jessie at the Des Forges' rambling house on Lafayette, but perhaps no house with such disappointing, healthy, Lexington Co-op-based snack offerings (other than my own house, that is). That yogurt sticks in my head.

But those snacks, I think, are just one of the many illustrations of Allison's radical, forward-thinking, responsible world view, and her way of seeing the big picture and making it personal. Like my own mom, (and Alison felt like a second mom to me for many years), Alison embraced the anti-corporate, organic, and sustainable, concepts that, decades later, still struggle for their rightful and necessary foothold. I remember, too, one of Jessie's birthdays, when Alison and Jessie requested only homemade gifts. I don't think I've ever taken as much pride, before or since, in gift-giving as I did over that handmade ballerina doll. It was a value, a lesson, an example.

I'm sure that others will focus on Alison's many and impressive contributions to the world and to justice in it. But for me, and undoubtedly for Jessie and Sandy's other friends and all the Montessori kids Alison worked with over the years, the striking thing was Alison's foresight for the importance of sharing her world with us, for passing her values on. Everyone is capable of going out and doing great things in this world, but it seems to me to be a rare thing to do that and to be a constant, real presence in the lives of children. By her example, Alison taught us how to live.

With love, gratitude, and profound sadness,

Molly Foran Yurchak

To the Des Forges family:

My heart hurts for you in your loss. Alison awed me without an ounce of intent.

As a young mother, who majored in Poli Sci because it was what drew, compelled and fascinated me; because I was interested in social justice, education and individual action, even on "big stuff", even when I felt small and unsure; Alison was an inspiration to me. I posted this earlier today:

Alison was an acquaintance whose quiet, calm, immovable dedication inspired me to accept and work hard to be elected and serve on the Buffalo Board of Education. She believed in commitment to human rights in so many facets—and she taught. It is a horrible loss of one of Buffalo's truly global/local citizens and leaders by example.

All the losses are painful, this one especially so, and I pray for comfort for the families, friends and our community in the remembering of each beautiful life.

Bless you all—

Sherry L. Byrnes

When I was about 15 years old, I decided to enter an essay contest. The contest required me to write an essay about an influential female. I thought of everyone I had ever met, and I decided to see if Alison Des Forges would allow me to interview her. She agreed to meet with me, and we set a time for me to come over to their house on Lafayette.

I went over and found Alison in a small room full of books that I believe was in the back of the house. I had prepared a series of questions for her, and expected that since she was so important she would only have about half an hour to talk to me.

During this period, Alison had just returned from working in Rwanda. When I asked her about her experience there, she held nothing back. She sat with me for two to three hours and told me everything there was to tell. She explained to me about the Hutus and the Tutsis, and she told me about the first occasion on which she saw mass graves that included children. I was shocked by what I heard, but I knew that this was a precious experience because she was telling me about important historical events that she had witnessed. I also quickly realized that I was in the presence of a true human rights hero. I felt blessed for the opportunity to be with her.

My essay didn't win the competition. I think most people chose to write about a famous woman like Harriet Tubman, or Gloria Steinem. Alison Des Forges was that kind of woman for me. As I proceeded through adolescence and faced many difficult choices, I sometimes made the wrong ones. I would occasionally see her around town, and she was a constant reminder of what it meant to be a good person. I consider her one of my personal heroes, and I believe that the time she spent with me changed my life and helped me see that helping others is what is most important in life. Now I am a high school teacher, and I can only hope to influence a few young people the way that she influenced me. I still teach about war and genocide and social control. This year, I will dedicate my teaching to her.

Susie Bartley

Youthful strength and zest, tempered by serious purpose....these are my impressions of Alison. I always noticed her on Elmwood, at the Co-Op, and was happy to share a world with such an important soul.

Trudy Stern

My appreciation goes now (and has, for a long time) to Alison and her family (especially Roger, whom I knew in History) for manifesting the power and possibilities women can bring to understanding and improving conditions of peoples through out the world. She was real in her dedicated service not only to those she served, but to those she inspired.

June Licence

I have only the vaguest memory of Alison. I remember her standing in front of a map at Bennett Park Montessori Center from one of her lessons on Africa. I can't have been more than six years old. What I remember most are her very kind eyes. While I can't bring up many specific details, I know that I owe her a lot, both as a founding parent of Montessori, and as a role model. I would not be the person I am without Montessori, or without the example of strong, educated women like Alison making a difference in the world. I only hope that all of us whose lives she touched can live up to her example.

Jessica Donnelly Reed

In 1994, Alison presented a program to Women's Action for New Directions about the horrific situation in Rwanda. Her compelling message prompted many letters to the UN and Congress. We will always remember her witness. WAND nationally continues to work for human rights and Peace.

Judy Metzger

Alison's profound impact on the world's understanding of the ongoing catastrophe in the Great Lakes and her unflinching demand for accountability will endure. Her fierce determination to speak truth to power will be sorely, painfully missed.

Colin Thomas-Jensen

Thank you, Alison, for your great courage and intelligence. Thank you for helping create the Montessori school which my daughter Nina soon attended. Thank you for your advocacy of public education. And thank you for being instrumental in having me added to the Capital Appropriations Committee for the City where I tried to help as much as possible.

My wife Beata, daughter Nina, and I offer our deepest condolences to Roger and to the entire family. After learning the news, we had our dinner at Elmwood's India Gate, the last place we had met Alison.

Paul Zarembka

Alison was an amazing human being. We are all so much better for having known her and so many people are better who never knew her personally.

I met Alison about 20 years ago. There is much known about her many incredible international human rights accomplishments but not so much about her effect locally in her home community of Buffalo, New York. Alison was one of the founders of Bennett Park Montessori School, one of very few public Montessori programs in the United States. Her dedication to public education then led her to form a city-wide parent organization to focus on systemic change in the public school district. Alison knew how to truly empower people by placing opportunities in front of them and letting them figure out how to accomplish their goals. She wouldn't do your work for you (after all, she had plenty of her own work to do!). Alison was hands-down the most brilliant woman I've ever met, yet she was no egotist and never expressed the hubris that often accompanies such brilliance. She merely expected everyone to function at her level and thereby acted as a role model and mentor for countless people.

Alison had a life changing impact on me many years ago. I am where I am and who I am today because of Alison. I will never forget attending one of the first meetings of United Parents in her home. At the end of the meeting people were milling around socializing when I approached Alison and introduced myself. I explained that I had some serious concerns about the lack of nurses in the Buffalo Public Schools. Alison looked at me with that piercing, attentive gaze that many would recognize, and she quietly told me, not in these exact words, that obviously I should start a health and safety committee to address my concerns. She was sure I could gather together some like-minded parents to work with me. And, you know, Alison was right. Our committee worked diligently for several years, getting Erie County to put more nurses in their budget. When we found out that school fire alarms were not hooked up to the fire department, we brought the issue before the Buffalo Board of Education to get the alarms hooked up. This all happened because Alison had an uncanny ability to recognize all that people were capable of doing and then expect them to do it. I know that there are many others with similar stories.

During the United Parents years under Alison's guidance and encouragement we were all speaking at and observing the board meetings on a regular basis. I remember one particular instance when Alison was addressing the board though I don't remember the specific issue at the time. As usual, Alison was speaking passionately and eloquently without any notes. (Since I had to have it all written down, including "my name is," this alone was an achievement that always amazed me.) During Alison's presentation the then-president of the board and one of his colleagues decided to have a quiet (not even whispered) conversation at the far end of the board table. Alison stopped speaking mid-word. It took less than a moment for the two rude board members to look up and receive Alison's wry comment, "Now that I have your attention, I will continue." And Alison launched, apparently seamlessly, back into her speech taking the board to task, I am sure, for whatever they were not doing to adequately and properly educate children in Buffalo. Alison's power was so tremendous because it was simply a part of her.

It is so very wrong that Alison left this earth too soon. My heart and healing thoughts are with Roger and Sandy and Jessie and their children. I keep telling myself that Alison will always live on in our memories and her great accomplishments have made a lasting impact on the world, but for me it's all too raw right now for that to be comforting.

Amy Melton (formerly Prentiss)

I have been summoning up the strength to write this tribute, and tears are blurring my vision as I type. Alison is irreplaceable at so many levels. Her departure is a terrible loss for Rwanda, the Great Lakes region, Africa and all who knew and worked with her.

As a former colleague in the Africa division at Human Rights Watch I was constantly inspired by Alison's combination of in-depth knowledge as an academic and activist commitment to making a difference. The two were inextricably linked: her ability to make a difference was fundamentally based on her knowledge of the history and politics of what she was talking about and skill in interpreting the issues to others. She spoke with the authority of interviews and insights gathered over decades, not just a single field trip. She was not only the peerless human rights expert on Rwanda and the Great Lakes, able to navigate and see a way to overcome the challenges of divided societies, but also consistently generous with her knowledge, never too important or too busy to share her wisdom. And always ready with a sardonic and slyly humorous comment to bring a misguided argument down to earth or to leaven the often grueling work.

I first got to know Alison when I became a researcher at HRW in the early 1990s. Then, from 6 April 1994, she suddenly went from being a member of the Africa division advisory board who had also contributed on an ad hoc basis to field research, to a 24-hour-a-day full time worker as the whole Africa team (small at that time) struggled to respond to the Rwanda genocide and focus international attention on what was going on. It was traumatic enough to be suddenly involved in that crisis work as someone who had never visited the country. Alison had close friends who were missing. Yet she was never impatient as I asked ignorant questions, and never let the worry and strain she was suffering hinder her efforts to lobby for the atrocity to receive the attention it was due. My admiration for her only grew the longer I worked for the organization.

Since I left HRW several years ago I have on several occasions been in touch with her for comments on a piece of writing, background on a person I was meeting, or input on a proposed project, and despite her busy schedule she always responded with insights I could not have obtained anywhere else. She is already in the acknowledgements of a book on citizenship in Africa I am just finalising. The least I can do is dedicate the book to her memory.

Many of us in human rights work can easily be substituted for someone else. Alison's place will never be filled.

In solidarity with her family and all my former HRW colleagues who knew and loved Alison.

Bronwen Manby

February 2009

Below is what I wrote for the HRW (Human Rights Watch) website:

To add to that—I can share my memories of the anecdote she often told of serving the court papers on Jean Bosco Barayagwiza, one of the genocidaires—which eventually resulted in a $100 million default judgment against him. He was attending the UN in late 1994, and staying in a hotel just outside the UN diplomatic zone (where he was out of US jurisdiction), walking distance from the HRW office near the NY Public Library. We (Alison and Holly Burkhalter and I) lurked in the hallway of the hotel, hiding behind our newspapers and trying to look inconspicuous, until he came through the lobby on the way back from the UN building. We weren't of course absolutely sure it was the right guy—despite Alison's encyclopaedic memory—so it was like a court room drama. 'Mr Barayagwiza?' 'Yes'. 'I am serving you with these papers from the New York District Court' - and she thrust the envelope into his hands. We then skedaddled and burst into giggles in the street with the release of tension. It was vintage Alison—as I later came to know—a highly serious purpose coupled with a wicked sense of the drama and fun of the moment.

I'm sorry I can't be with you for the service. Given the way that I am feeling I cannot imagine how the family is coping. I never met them, but please give them my love.

I first met Alison when she was a mother of two young children who were attending a small Montessori school in downtown Buffalo housed at St Mary of

Sorrows convent. The Director of the school, Eileen Buermann, was working with a group of her parents who envisioned this model as an alternative within the Buffalo Public Schools so children and parents from all over Buffalo would be able to have the opportunity to have their children attend a Montessori program.

This group approached the Board of Education and began working with Rae Rosen, a supervisor in the schools and Irene Murphy, a director at Nardin Montessori, among others, to create a plan make this program possible.

I attended a meeting that was held to find out what this Montessori program was all about and heard from parents and Eileen about this unique way of teaching children. Their energy was contagious and subsequently several Buffalo teachers started working on Saturdays at Nardin as part of a two year process to become Montessori certified so we could open this school.

Bennett Park Montessori opened in 1977 as a part of the court order to desegregate the Buffalo Public Schools.

Alison continued her relationship with Bennett Park as an active parent volunteering in the school, making materials that are still used today, organizing field trips for students and in-servicing the faculty. She worked getting other parents involved and encouraged everyone to take an active role in the school.

We knew that she and her husband, Roger were actively involved in their own research and they went as a family to China and Africa during these years. As Jessie and Sandy moved on to high school, she kept in touch sometimes bringing people who were staying with her to school. We knew that Alison was playing a significant role in Rwanda and as part of Human Rights Watch but we continued to know her as a proud mother and grandmother as her family grew.

The world is a better place because of Alison Des Forges and because she committed herself to making it a better place, thousands of students over the thirty years that Bennett Park has existed as a Buffalo Public School, have benefited from her work. Thank you, Alison.

Jan Dombkowski

For Alison

if I knew you were leaving before springtime
even before the snowdrops
if I knew you would travel away within an enormous scarlet star
that touched the earth long enough to take you
I would have thanked you for teaching me
I would have told you
I never speak of a family's home
as a shack or a hut
I would have said I always tell my students
where Rwanda is
I tell them you have to crouch down
avert your eyes   stay quiet   out of respect for the gorillas
who live in the emerald mountains there
I would thank you because
I see beauty differently now
because of the long ago books you shared
the ones whose photographs we looked at over and over
the pieces of lives we learned
Masai warriors scribing patterns along their legs
in the red mud of their land
women from other African countries who paint their milky homes

with the palette of earth from their villages

see their homes washed by rain and repaint them

I would thank you for opening us all

for opening Rwanda   Africa   the world

with your thoughtful words

I would tell you we carry them still

like a moonflower wide open glowing

the enormous fire of your star is gone

you are the constellation of peace

the silvery trail of light

gleaming sapphire in our new winter sky

we wish for you

long for the snowdrops

the first stars we will touch in spring

Barbara Q. Faust
Friday February 13, 2009

While the world knew Alison Des Forges as a tireless and accomplished protector of human rights, I knew her as the mother of one of my close childhood friends, Sandy Des Forges. Matt, my younger brother, was best friends with Sandy. By day we all attended Buffalo's first public Montessori school, Bennett Park Montessori Center, and on weekends and in the afternoons we would frequently get together with Sandy. We played street football, rode our bicycles and spent hours building huge spacecrafts from the enormous collection of Legos at the Des Forges home. When we played at Sandy's house Alison was there to watch over us and provide a hungry brood of kids with snacks. From time to time we would stay for a special meal, often an authentic Chinese recipe few would experience outside of China.

As school was Montessori, we frequently undertook large projects where we studied multiple facets of the same topic. Notable among these were studying Africa and China where as a class we created books covering a wide variety subjects about each region. Of course Alison was the driving force behind these projects with her incredible knowledge of these far off places. One day she would talk to us about the major rivers on the continent, and the next day she would teach us about music and the musical instruments they played in Rwanda. As a scholar she knew so much, and as a mother she wanted to teach it to us.

As a child I saw Alison as a mother who cherished that role, and as someone who really was a genius – even as a kid it was impossible to know Alison and not realize that she was one of the most intelligent people you would ever meet in your life.

It was not until I heard the tragic news of Alison's passing that I stepped back and reflected upon the woman I knew. All the information available talked of Alison's tremendous professional accomplishments as a human rights advocate and authority on central Africa . It did not surprise me to hear of the things Alison had done after I knew her, and it made me wonder how anyone, particularly an academic of small physical stature, could have the capacity for caring and face the dangers she faced in the name of doing what is right. I'm not sure I'll ever figure out how someone could do the things Alison did.

Long before Alison made an impact on a world stage she made an impact locally, and that's what I'll remember because it directly impacted me. Alison was a driving force in the creation of Bennett Park Montessori – without her I don't believe the school would have ever been created. Alison, with others like Eileen Buermann, willed BPMC into being and we all benefitted. It is hard for me to imagine what a different path I would be on today had my grade school years been spent in a traditional classroom rather than a Montessori program. I am tremendously proud to be a member of BPMC's first graduating class, the first product of such a wonderful school.

For every person in Africa Alison helped, let us not forget her tremendous accomplishments locally and all the lives she touched in Buffalo. To think that BPMC is but a footnote in her life's achievements shows how much of an impact Alison had as a human being. People who touch the world so positively and profoundly are few and far between, and I am honored that I had the opportunity to know one of them in Alison Des Forges.

Tony Bogyo
Chelmsford, MA

I have so many wonderful memories of the years I knew Alison but here are just a few:
* St. Mary's Montessori School when our kids were 3 and 4 years old
* Bennett Park Montessori—the work she did to make it happen
* Winter camp-outs at Franklinville
* Snowshoeing and tubing with the kids
* The Africa projects and the China projects
* The bird walks and identification projects
* Sleeping under the stars on a hill above the Franklinville camp in the spring
* Sandy and Matt and the huge spacecraft and fort they built in the Des Forges backyard
* The night Matt slept through the firemen rushing to check out a chimney fire at the Des Forges' house

* Evenings and weekends making materials for teachers to use at Bennett Park Montessori

* Building the playground behind the school

* Time spent together at our cottage on Cape Cod one summer

* Irish dancing classes after school, taught by Alison

* Chinese food—and especially Chinese meatballs—prepared by Alison

* Many cups of tea on the side, front or back steps on Lafayette Ave

* Birthday parties for each of the kids

The loss of such a caring and energetic person will be felt by so many for so long. I thank heaven that I knew her and feel truly blessed to have shared some of her life for all those years! I will always think of her and remember the good times!

Sincerely,
Janneke Bogyo

I was best friends with Alison's son Sandy from kindergarten up to 7th grade. I have great memories of spending time at their house on weekends and also of all the fun activities that Alison did with us at school. We were the first class to go through the Montessori program and were lucky enough to be the first ones to make a giant salt map of Africa and build a Rwandan hut in the gym. I still have my copy of the Africa book that I made in 1st grade. I currently am an Associate Professor at Stanford and I work on discovery of new drug targets to treat malaria so in many way my life has come full circle back to an interest in Africa. My kids Ben and Sophia (age 4 and 6) both went to Montessori pre-school. Every time I go into their classroom and see the trinomial cube exercise I did as I kid, I cannot help but think back to Bennett Park Montessori and all the great teachers we had there. I feel really lucky not only to have had Alison as a teacher, but also to have been able to spend so much time in her home as kid. Both she and Roger always made me feel so welcome and part of the family. She will be greatly missed but the legacy of all that she has done will certainly live on. I know she had a big impact on my life.

Sincerely,

Matt Bogyo

Waaaaaay back when the Buffalo Public School System was working on the African Infusion Project, to infuse African and African American content into the curriculum, Alison was one of the consultants. Working with her was always a pleasure. She was competent, knowledgeable, kind, generous, and personable. I loved her smile!

Karima Amin

I first met Alison when Jessie and I were running track together at City Honors. I lived a few blocks from the Des Forges, and Alison was always kind enough to offer me a ride home from the track when she picked up Jessie. The generosity and kindness that Alison showed when I was in high school extended to each and every interaction I have had with her since.

I went to Haverford a year behind Jessie, and in 1994 decided to write my final paper for an ethnic conflict class on Rwanda. I hadn't known that Alison was an expert on Rwanda until Jessie suggested I call her for some pointers on the paper.

Alison exhibited a rare kindness, patience, and indulgence of all my elementary questions as she spoke with me on the phone for over an hour. She didn't just answer my questions; she shared her profoundly personal experiences in Rwanda and experiences with Rwandan friends who had suffered during the conflict. That conversation is partly responsible for what would eventually be my very Africa-focused career. Alison described a region gripped by both horror and beauty—a country where the worst of humanity could easily be seen, but where the best of humanity could also be found if you looked hard enough. Listening to the stories from her work helped me realize the tough but meaningful opportunities that existed for anyone interested in making a difference.

During my work in DC and at the State Department, I have continued to cross paths with Alison on occasion, and she has been an inspiration to me and several of my colleagues. She was truly a model intellectual, activist, and upholder of all that is moral and just. She leaves an incredible void that will be felt by more people than I can imagine.

Sarah Skorupski

I wrote this the Saturday after the horrific news of Friday, the 12th of February. Eileen thought it might be appropriate to share. Alison was an extraordinary person and I was on the receiving end of her enormous kindness several times. I wanted to honor her spirit and the loss of all the families and friends touched by the devastation of that day.

In Memory of Alison Des Forges   *February 12, 2009*

     Fiery crash

     Inferno shooting straight

     Up

Such destruction

Such merciless disintegration of what

Was   just seconds before

In the high Andes Q'ero elders burn their prayers

Breathe each prayer into an earthly form...a petal, a twig...

Reverently wrap them in paper   colors of the rainbow

Bring them to the fire

For   release

Water is the language of our body

Body thirsts for its purification

Body follows its tides

Spirit speaks a different language

Fire is its tongue

Transformation its thirst

Who am I   then

Who were they   really

We're brought unwillingly to the fire

A foreign place, a language we don't speak

But spirit feels at home   at last

It shoots straight up

Releasing its prayers

 Courage Kindness Generosity Exuberance Gratitude

So that what was living in one human heart

May fly free to the hearts of many

My Friend Alison

Paula Schenk

Life brings to all of us, fortune and misfortune; even tragedy to some. I was graced with such fortune by being able to work with Alison Des Forges. Bennett Park Montessori Center started with a small cadre of teachers. I was one of them. Alison was a parent of two children at the school, a promoter and developer of the school and a daily volunteer in the school building. This week, I've been experiencing flashbacks of visual venues with Alison. My memories of Alison always float on a peaceful cloud. When I was in the presence of Alison, I was as George Costanza stated, "in serenity now." Alison could lower your blood pressure just by looking at you with those clear blue eyes and her head slightly tilted. When you talked to Alison, Alison was there for you. At that moment, you were the only person that mattered. Your thoughts were important to her even if she disagreed. Alison was brave and strong enough to tell you always with respect that your thoughts were not her viewpoint. I admired her for her strength to share her differing opinion.

My flashbacks are not so much of Alison talking but of Alison listening. I reminisce many scenarios with Alison and Eileen, our Montessori trainer and another co-founder of the school. Alison is always looking at Eileen with such admiration. Alison's intent for the successful development of the school was focused and serious. She wanted to be a part of laying a strong foundation. She looked at Eileen, as the Montessori expert and cheered Eileen on as well as the rest of the staff, parents and teachers.

Her quiet and strong presence was evident with the children. I see her taking the hand of a rambunctious child and looking at him or her. It was that look of wisdom and connection. She was telling the child without words, "we talked about this behavior before and this is the time to check your behavior and be peaceful."

Alison was so generous with her time. She shared many days and hours with the children at Bennett Park Montessori Center. Her projects and stories of Africa were all a part of the school community. Who could forget the giant three dimensional map of Africa constructed by the children under her direction in the Common Hall of the school? It was created and designed with such love and respect for the continent and its people.

On a personal level, sometimes I was fortunate to eat lunch with Alison in the Meeting Place of the school. Alison was also generous in sharing her quick wit and we did have some chuckles. At our lunch encounters, Alison talked about her family with delight. She shared that life gave her so much pleasure in giving her a loving family. She was grateful for her husband and children. Both of us were not born or bred in Buffalo. However, she convinced me that I would consider Buffalo my hometown someday. It was Alison's theory that Buffalo is the place I will grow to love because this is where I will raise my family. Alison possessed a wisdom of love too.

I realize that certain people enter my earthly life with a lesson to teach me. I am so fortunate to be attentive to Alison's lesson for me, "Love what you do, do what you love and do it without ego." Alison, may you rest in heavenly peace. I know you'll always be with me.

With Respect and Love,
Stephanie Gregorie

Alison Des Forges— February 12, 2009

I met Alison and Roger as parents of two beautiful children, Sandy and Jessie, at St. Mary of Sorrows Montessori School – Sandy, you were 4 years old. This program was a unique scholarship program with an alternative educational system. This is where the seeds were planted for Montessori to grow into the public system through a magnet program as a way to integrate the public schools. In 1976 Judge Curtin said that we need to come up with a plan to desegregate Buffalo schools. How fortunate that Alison was there as a community activist who was not afraid to ask the difficult questions.

In September 1977, Bennett Park Montessori Center opened as one of the early Public Montessori schools in the United States and Alison made so many contributions through her daily volunteering not just for Jessie and Sandy, but always for all the children.

Alison, we are thankful for all that you did. You organized and made many presentations to the school board to provide this alternative for ALL children, to invite and recruit parents, to recruit, select and welcome future faculty. You modeled for us how to begin research with three year olds by looking at cultural pictures. You prepared many groups of children to make oral presentations and debates in social studies. You researched and prepared a multipage history of holidays for us on your faithful typewriter so that we can celebrate the holidays around the world instead of just using the commercial point of view. I still use this in the Montessori training program.

You sensitized us not to use a variety of words like "tribe" for a group of people and the word "hut" as a word to describe someone's home. I can remember saying, but Alison, it is a three letter phonetic word—that's a Montessori language joke—yes, we removed it with an understanding and sensitivity. You built 12' x 12' maps of Africa and Asia out of plywood in the common hall with groups of children. Then the children painted the land and water forms - rivers and mountain ranges.

Alison, you supported our developmental camping trips beginning with seven year olds to Whispering Pines in Franklinville—a program that is still happening today.

You prepared and introduced many children to a variety of cultures through field trips to museums. For example, we visited the Royal Ontario Museum in Toronto for an exquisite Chinese exhibit. To the Strong Museum in Rochester when we were studying the Gilded Ages. This was the time in history when train transportation was developing, and so we traveled on a train. The children were excited and the docents were impressed with the knowledge the children brought with them.

As Helene Kramer wrote, "You were an advocate for people who could not advocate for themselves," not just in Western New York but around the world.

Alison, our world needs you so badly now; your work will be missed; your dedication will be missed; your energy, drive, humility, passion, thoughts, insights, warmth, your smile are gone forever.

Our conversations always ended with a semicolon; to be picked up where we left off, till the next time we would meet, but now we have reached a period. Roger, Sandy, and Jessie, may we still have a semicolon in our conversations in our future.

I would like to leave you with a Maria Montessori quote that personifies Alison's work which leads us to a better world for all humanity. "Not in the service of any political or social creed should the teacher work, but in the service of the complete human being able to exercise in freedom a self-diciplined will and judgment unperverted by prejudice and undistorted by fear." (*To Educate the Human Potential*)

Eileen Buermann

I have very fond memories of Bennett Park, and I think of those times often. And I remember Alison (yes, retaining the convention of calling adults by first names) very well. I think everyone from that time tells the story about building the floor-sized map of Africa in the gym. I've told countless people over the years about that map—and of Alison's prominent place in such a unique school. I remember Alison taking us to a local African art museum, and Roger visiting to show us how to paint Chinese figures in black ink. I also remember Sandy and Jessie going with their parents to live in Africa. Funny, those memories inform so much of what I value most. It's one thing to read about far off places and different cultures and peoples, or to study maps and pictures on a wall; it's quite another to feel and touch and experience things up close and in person. I think that's the key to Alison's impact on me—I believe she knew children have an unlimited capacity to learn. Of all the tributes to her accomplishments, she will be for me a "teacher." I'm very grateful to have been a part of Bennett Park at its founding and in the company of such an extraordinary woman.

Jennifer Collesano Adams
(Bennett Park Montessori, 1977-82)

Some Memories of Alison

It's hard to write about Alison – there is so much to say, and yet nothing I can say is at all adequate. The following are a few of my many memories of and thoughts about Alison, in the order in which they occur to me.

My memories of Alison are all mixed together with memories of all the great times I had with Jessie as a child. Roller skating up and down the block on Lafayette. Going to Orchard Park to see the Des Forges' relatives. Sleeping over at the Des

Forges' house. Jessie and Sandy would get up early and get into bed with Alison and Roger to snuggle.

Highland dancing. Alison was a champion highland dancer! She taught me and Jessie the highland fling.

We danced to the Nutcracker Suite in the living room. The record player in the corner at the bottom of the stairs.

When we were carefully (or not so carefully) trying to move a piece of furniture, I learned the phrase "Easy does it," from Alison. When we carried something upstairs from the basement, Alison said "Jessie is a very strong child," and Jessie added loyally, "Rachel is a very strong child too!"

We had so many, many happy times together when Jessie, Sandy and I were little. They stayed in Vicky Weisskopf's house in the summer. During one or more summers, Jessie and I went to Drumlin Farm camp together, and we swam at Valley Pond, and at camp we skipped down the hill singing *"Il e'tait un petit navire"* ("There was a little ship") together.

My mother, Sukey, wrote little stories about the "Fes Dorges." I forget whether she cut up the story into strips that had to be fit together like a puzzle, or dropped off installments of the stories in their mailbox; maybe both.

Alison had several of Sukey's recipes, I think. Lemon cake and also some others.

When Sukey was in the last few months of her illness, Alison came over to our house a lot. I remember one day I felt a tickle at my waist. I thought it was just my clothing or something I had brushed against, and I ignored it. Then I felt another tickle and turned, and it was Alison, who had somehow come in silently.

I don't exactly know what exactly Alison did, but I felt that during Sukey's last months of illness and for the first year or two after she died, Alison was one of the people who really, really looked out for me, took care of me, made sure I was okay, showed me what friends can do for each other, gave me the model for friendship – I don't know exactly how to say it, but Alison was just such a good friend at that time when I was so much in need of help and friendship. I feel forever grateful even though I don't remember precisely what she did. I just know that I have felt, and feel, so much gratitude.

When I was a bit older, I saw a card for sale at Positively Main Street that I wanted to buy for Alison. It showed a picture of a teacher in front of a group of students, and the caption was "May you have as much happiness as you bring to others." I don't think I ever got to buy the card, but I am pretty sure that I summoned the courage to write Alison a note – maybe around Christmas – in which I quoted the card.

The year the Des Forges were in Rwanda, I think I was eight, so Jessie was about seven and Sandy about nine. Jessie and I exchanged letters. Alison typed long letters and sent them to her mother, Sybil, who xeroxed them and sent them out to a big group of friends. Jessie played singing and dancing games with other girls, and I think the Des Forges had a goat. At the time I knew the names of her friends there; one was Fatima, I think. They drove through fearsome pot-holed roads – maybe this was when they went to see the gorillas. I remember the description of the roads, in her letter. Maybe the car even got stuck in a pot hole, or threatened to break down, along the way.

When the family spent a year in China, on their return, Jessie and Sandy had lost their Buffalo accents and pronounced their A's differently for a while. Jessie had gotten very strong from being in a ballet class where the students had to hold their legs up (out straight) for long periods of time. Jessie and Sandy both came back speaking Chinese, and Jessie sang funny little Chinese opera snippets with accompanying hand motions.

When we were younger, the neighbors taught us the song, *"Alle Voegel sind schon da; alle Voegel, alle."* (All the birds have come/returned; all the birds, all.)

With Roger, we sang, *"Dites moi pourquoi la vie est belle; dites moi pourquoi la vie est gaie; dites moi pourquoi, chere demoiselle—est-ce que c'est parce que vous m'aimez?"* (Tell me why life is beautiful; tell me why life is gay; tell me why, dear maiden – is it because you love me?)

Roger read us "Twinkletoes," in a quiet voice, sitting on the futon by the fire place.

I have just always loved Alison so much.

Alison was always thinking of people I should meet or talk to or be connected to in some way. In college, when my advisor for a summer research project fell through at the last minute, I told Alison and she asked Claude Welch to be my advisor. She put me in touch with old friends who had moved to Chicago—Jupp and Karin and their two daughters. I have the name Cyrie Sendashonga written in my address book – someone Alison wanted me to call, in Montreal. In Princeton, Trish Hiddleston. Just a few of the many, many people Alison introduced me to, or told me to call, at various times and places.

There's a story in Jewish tradition about the "lamed vav tsadikim"—often translated as the thirty-six "righteous" people. Thirty-six is twice eighteen, and the number eighteen matches the spelling for the word for life, so thirty-six is twice-times-life. The idea is that there are thirty-six particularly good people in the world at any given time. I like to say that thirty-six must have been the estimate that corresponded to the earth's population back in the early days of humanity, but that clearly that number has risen in tandem with the exponential growth in the human population, because otherwise, how could I know so many of those particularly good people personally! Alison is one of the people I am always thinking of when I say that.

Dropping by the Des Forges' house. Ringing the bell, then going to peer in the big window to see if anybody appeared. Or sometimes, just tapping on the window, in order not to bother them if they were upstairs. Or in summer, going around to the back yard; maybe Alison would be sitting on the back stairs, talking on the phone with the cord stretching into the kitchen, past the laundry machine and the cat food. Or try the side door. Sukey would always go in the side door and call "hello!" up the stairs, rather than try to figure out whether the door bell was working that day.

When the genocide began in Rwanda, Alison was working night and day trying to save people. At first she couldn't sleep, and then when she did begin to sleep a little, she woke Roger up because she was gripping his arm so hard in her sleep.

When we were little, Alison taught us various things at school. We made a book about Native Americans, a book about Africa, and a book about China. (I know Alison did the Africa and China parts, and I think she did the part about Native Americans, but I'm not certain of that.)

For the China project, we worked in pairs, and each pair had a word to look up in the encyclopedia. Amy Rabin and I were responsible for looking up the word lacquer. What a strange word! I've felt special ownership of it ever since. I remember the moment of entering the library to look up our word: lacquer.

We also learned some Chinese calligraphy. Sukey did a science project with us around the same time, on water drops and surface tension (studying water drops on waxed paper).

For the Africa book, our topic was Dan masks. We learned about how the types of masks were distinguished from one another by the shape of the eyes and other features.

When Alison came to Princeton to give a talk, and I was sitting at dinner later with her and a group of maybe twelve other people, I had this thought. Modern

Christianity focuses on the concept of Jesus being both human and divine. In some earlier versions of Christianity, there was more emphasis on the mix of the human and the divine in everyone. Over dinner, watching Alison, I suddenly understood that concept. I thought of a cake mixture – maybe the egg ingredients in one bowl and the chocolate ingredients in another bowl, and you pour one mixture into the other and they form all these beautiful swirls. I saw the mixture of the human and the divine as I watched Alison. I see it sometimes in other people, since then, but that was the first time it occurred to me that way.

Writing down these memories, I'm overwhelmed by all the different directions my thoughts take. Thinking about how Alison's work in Rwanda is well known, but do people also know about her work to support public schools. Thinking about Alison's beautiful face and her wide cheekbones, and how when she traveled to Czechoslovakia she was struck by the fact that people there looked like her; she'd never been among people who looked like her before. Thinking about the blue silk skirt and shirt that she wore at Jessie's wedding. Thinking about how she started having to talk to the media all the time, and how I was visiting one day and someone called her for a TV interview so she had to quickly find some business togs to put on for the camera. How her phone was ringing constantly all day and night so they finally got a separate phone number for family to use. Walking over to Kinko's to send faxes and make xeroxes. Thinking about Alison's friendship with Helene and their thousands of walks around Delaware Park.

The attic – the playroom, and the mystery room we weren't really supposed to go into, and Alison and Roger's little office, where Sandy put out a newspaper about happenings on their block, such as when the police were somehow called by mistake during a game of kids spraying each other with a hose at Savannah and Clay's house; and where Alison then wrote all her massive documentation of the Rwandan genocide, or before that, other reports for Human Rights Watch. When she finished her book, she wasn't going to put her name on it, but Ann, among others, convinced her to.

When Alison saw one of her friends in Rwanda after the genocide, the friend asked Alison how Jessie and Sandy (now Alex) were doing. Alison said they were doing well, and showed her friend some pictures. Her friend said, "I don't even have pictures of my children."

Alison offered to have one of her friend's surviving children, Celestin, come to live with her and Roger, and to send him to school in the U.S. So he came and lived with Alison and Roger for a number of years and became an adopted member of the family. Later his sister Josee came too.

Alison said a few years ago that she had thought of something she wanted to give me—I think she said, "I thought of a perfect birthday present for you." I never found out what it was.

One time, when I was little, Alison came over when I was having a bath, and she took charge of my bath for a few minutes. She asked if I made sculptures with my hair when it had shampoo in it. Apparently Jessie did this all the time—I didn't know! Meaning, when your hair is wet and full of shampoo suds, you make sculptures with it on the top of your head.

Thinking about Alison's face, soft skin, slippers, her walk, her hugs, her interest, her questions, a glass of juice from the fridge, a cup of tea, the house I know so well, the cone-topped African baskets, the pendulum toy on the window sill (you swing one silver ball and it sends the momentum through to the one on the other side). Playing *iggisauro*—the game with beans/beads—first the relatively simple version of the game with two rows, then the more comjplicated version with four rows. Jumping on Roger and Alison's bed; playing with Kristin and Kaitlin next door.

At Jessie's birthday party one year, we played "running the gauntlet," in which the children stand in two rows facing each other and one child walks down the middle; the other kids try to make him or her laugh, and he or she tries not to laugh. We also played (same concept) "poor pussy," in which the kids sit in a circle and one child is the pussy cat, who goes around to each child in turn and tries to make him or her laugh. The kids in the circle have to pat the pussy cat child on the head and say "poor pussy." Whichever child laughs takes the next turn as the pussy cat.

Jessie and I used to play giggle pots. We would just say "let's be giggle pots," and we would start to laugh and laugh, didn't have to have any particular specific thing to laugh about.

When we all went for a bike ride, Alison rode in front, then the kids, and Roger brought up the rear. They explained it was like the way ducks travel—Alison in front like the mother duck, us following like ducklings, Roger at the end like a father duck.

Sitting in the living room, talking, with a cup of tea.

Alison and Roger always called each other "Dear." I think on some occasions they gave each other cards, "To Dear #1," "from "Dear #2."

Having dinner at the Des Forges'. Sitting next to Jessie and giggling. Each person with his or her special napkin in a napkin ring.

At St. Mary's of Sorrows, we learned to sing this prayer before meals: "For health and friends and daily bread, we praise thy name, oh lord." Sandy changed it to include happiness, so at the Des Forges' house we sang, "For health, food, friends and happiness we praise thy name oh lord."

Lemonade at the Des Forges' house. Christmas tree with books underneath. Sandy with his chin on his knees, reading *The New York Times*.

Alison's voice on the phone—"Hi Rache!"

I cannot imagine Buffalo without Alison.

I've always looked up to Alison, wanted to meet her standards, wanted to live up to my own potential in a way and to an extent that Alison would approve of.

When I was little, I thought that Sandy and Jessie went to sleep every night at eight and woke up every morning at eight (and maybe in fact they did?!)—and I aspired to live up to that standard (though I think I also despaired of ever succeeding).

Several of us walked to an event or exhibition in some Buffalo neighborhood one evening. I mentioned, or someone mentioned, that it was not considered a safe area to walk at night. Alison considered this ridiculous, and we went ahead and walked.

Running up and down the two flights of stairs – the carpeted stairs and the wood stairs. The one spot in the stained glass window mosaic where the glass was missing, a secret, stopping to look and find the space that was covered up with tape.

Watching Alison speak at the podium – how she spoke so fluently, passionately, and by heart, didn't seem to need notes.

If I had to pick one thing to say about Alison – no, it would have to be two things – If I had to pick two, or three, things, to save in my heart about Alison – Well, but I don't have to choose.

One day – this was when Jessie was pregnant with Alexa, I think—I had some things I was worrying about, fretting about, and then I sorted through my worries, got over it, and I went to Jessie and Dan's for dinner, with Alison and Roger, it was summer, and we ate outside in the back yard, and I was filled with a sense of how beautiful the world was that evening.

What I've written here are some snapshots, some tiny snippets of much bigger memories. I haven't really written about how I feel about Alison, about the role she's played in my life, about how it feels to me to lose her. I haven't written about the principles that Alison has stood up for, that I've taken for granted as a reference point in so many situations. There might be a way to say, in a few words, something about the warm feeling of being with Alison, just how happy it makes one to be in her presence. The Human Rights Watch article about her captures in words something about Alison's sense of humor, the twinkle in her eye. I don't think it captures Alison's amazing ability to tell stories, and the expressiveness of her eyebrows. I can't even begin to think about what it will mean to not have Alison here in Buffalo, filling up the city with her presence, even while off on travels hither and yon.

Alison told me at one point that after what she'd seen in Rwanda, she'd lost her sense of fear—or at least, she'd lost any fear of flying. She had been in a very bumpy flight on the way home, in which many of the passengers were very frightened, and she wasn't afraid at all.

There is so much to say about Alison, and I wish there were no reason to be writing it down. Since I have to stop writing somewhere, I'll end with this: Alison has always been an ideal for me, a measure to live up to, and at the same time, a source of confidence. Alison is one of the people who has taught me what a wonderful thing friendship can be, at a time when it's most needed.

I think about whether there's a formula for living a life as good as Alison's, and I am pretty sure that there isn't. But to know Alison is to know how good a life can be. The amazing people you read about in books, who rescue others in the subtlest or the bravest ways, are not just in books. They are right here. How to live up to Alison's standards –I don't know for sure, but one thing I think of is when you can see what is needed, what's the right thing, not to bother about hesitating, just feel free to do it.

I think about Alison's voice on the phone and her warm greeting, coming to answer the door.

Rachel Massey

Alison Des Forges died last week in a plane crash just outside of Buffalo, New York. But that's probably about the least important part of her extraordinary life.

Alison meant a lot of things to a lot of people. I'm going to be selfish for a few minutes and write about what she meant and continues to mean to me:

Alison was a gifted storyteller, an invaluable mentor, an inspirational teacher, a great cook, and my second mom. She's the woman who taught me by example about honor, respect, focus, humility, and personal discipline.

She also taught me how to use chopsticks. She started me out on chunks of chicken and veggies. Then it was grapes. Then raisins. Then little scraps of shelled peanuts. (I asked her if she'd teach me how to pluck individual eyelashes off a gnat. She said she wasn't sure gnats had eyelashes.)

When I was nine, she helped my class build an enormous map of Africa out of wood, wire mesh, paste, paint, and *papier-mache.* She never stopped trying to open our eyes.

Alison believed that justice was more about hard work, persistence, and faith than it was about retribution and compromise for the sake of political expediency. Sometimes, when I got tired, I remembered Alison's unflagging energy. (The rest of us get twenty-four hours per day. Alison somehow managed to get in thirty.) When I doubted myself, when I felt small as David, I remembered how Alison never ever stopped trying to bring down Goliath.

We had many wonderful conversations in the thirty-some years I knew her. Through her words, I sometimes heard terrible things. Human suffering. Inhuman atrocities. I heard about one of the many trips she made to Rwanda to document the genocide when she recounts not being able to walk through one particular church without stepping on human bodies. In her voice I heard determination. Sorrow. Frustration. Anger.

And hope. Always hope.

Through her eyes, I saw the world.

She was brilliant not because of the amount she knew (which was considerable) but because of her capacity for compassion, her ferocity of spirit, her work ethic, and her ability to listen to a million people speaking at once. All those voices the rest of us tune out – she heard. She could read a silly story to one of her grandchildren, then kneel down at Montessori and listen to a five year old tell her about his drawing of his family. Then she could stand up and listen to me talk about my writing. Then she could fly halfway around the world and listen to a devastated nation screaming for peace and justice. And she managed to give her full attention to each person all the time.

Count yourself lucky if you got to have a single conversation with Alison. If you got to see those animated eyebrows jumping around and those blue eyes of hers flash fire. If you got to hear her tell a story, laugh at a joke, or just sit and listen as you spoke. When I talked to her, she made me feel like what I had to say was important. Like I was important. But not in a way that made me feel arrogant. Just competent. Like I was at my best. Like I mattered.

In one of the last conversations I ever had with her, I thanked her for being there for me when I needed the most help in my life and for inspiring me through her marriage and through her commitment to human rights to believe in myself and in my capacity to be the father my kids needed and the husband my wife deserved. I'll always be glad we had that conversation, and I'm glad I told her what she meant to me. (Oh, and I once asked her at her house if she wanted me to set a dessert place for her. She said, "I'll just have mine in Roger's lap." I said, "Wouldn't you rather eat out of a plate?" And we burst out laughing. At last she said, "I'm fifty years old, and I'm blushing!" and we all laughed some more. So I made her laugh and blush, and we shared a cute and funny moment, and I'm kind of glad about that, too.)

You see, miracles do happen. Alison's husband got to be with one for fifty years. Her two extraordinary children got to call one of those miracles "Mom." They don't feel like it right now, but to me, they're the luckiest people I've ever met.

God gets to have a chance to know her now. I don't know if there are conflicts in Heaven, but if so, God's got the ultimate warrior-diplomat by his side. He just better not piss her off.

I'm supposed to tell Alison to rest in peace, but I won't. She was already always at peace, even when she had her ears back and her teeth bared as she fought against those who would deprive peace to others. And she never ever rested.

The world may be full of misery, but it was also full of Alison. No one who met her can doubt that heroes exist.

Malcolm Watson

Words Spoken at the Memorial

Maggid Andrew Gold

We've all come here today to honor our beloved Susan. And the very size of this turn-out is such an honoring in itself. But what does it really mean to honor someone who has passed on? What does the tradition imply when it says: "Zakor tzaddik l'vracha"—the memory of the righteous will be for blessing. How do we make remembrance a blessing? One of the ways is by being inspired by a beloved one's special qualities, and striving to reflect those qualities into the world within the truthful mirror of our own beings. By doing that, our remembrance extends the chain of blessing from our loved one into the future that her earthly eyes will not see.

Cantors are often taught to sing from the diaphragm. Susan sang from the heart. You may not be able to sing like Susan, but you can sing as Susan sang. And God knows this world needs song.

We've all been touched by Susan's extraordinary compassion—her deep caring for people in their many places of suffering. We honor Susan through our own acts of compassion.

Susan marvelled at God's creation, and she was so excited and grateful to see that green and black and red Toucan in a nature preserve in Costa Rica two days before her death. Honor Susan's memory by being a passionate protector of God's holy creation.

Susan loved and celebrated the diversity of humanity and its religious traditions, as witnessed by this gathering today. Honor Susan by learning about the 'other', by learning to love that 'other'. She was so deeply agonized by the suffering of both Israelis and Palestinians, even as one of her beloved sons, Jonah, was forced to take shelter from falling rockets in Be'er Sheva. And she spoke eloquently in honor of both peoples' legitimacies.

She had recently begun to study about Islam, and was helping craft a Jewish /Christian / Muslim youth program here in Buffalo. Honor Susan by supporting such a vision, as she knew that all our children's future depends on it.

Susan was such a God-lover. And she lived with a passion for the wisdom and beauty of her beloved Judaism, and its call to a life of truthful service. She learned and went deep, and inspired others to kindle the flame of their own passion. Honor Susan by kindling your own flame, which kindles that of others.

And we know Susan as being so courageous. And she certainly was. But she also carried great fears for much of her life. It was her courage and will that allowed her to push past those fears, to not allow her fears to limit her zeal to taste life fully. I have been gifted to witness her continually stretching past her fears as we traveled together over the past years and during this past week.

We honor Susan by refusing to be limited by the fears we each carry. If each of us still gifted with the breath of Life will truly embrace that gift during the precious moments yet allotted to us, our memory of this sweet and wise and willing Tzaddik will truly be for blessing.

3407

Marek Parker

The sky is falling! The sky is falling!

yell jaundiced news men and women

as they turn grief into shame

hunched over embers

    stoking flames with hourly updates

A catastrophe, a horror, late breaking news

    brings sympathy, sadness, and ratings points

Exploring sorrow

    well past its saturation

earning points from the community

    all the while abusing their trust

Insufficient training

    pilot error

sleep deprivation

    airlines just looking at the profits

Self proclaimed leaders

    rise to the front

comforting the pained with a pat on the back

    while waving to the cameras with the other hand

Ministers profit from increased exposure
    daily prayers and announcements
    as bulbs burst in ready face
their Jesus seems to need a photo op

Lawyers skirt around the 30 day no solicitation rule
"contacting" families to express their shared grief
while lining up clients in the name of despair

monuments,memorials, memories
    who can erect the biggest

This carnage is like mother's milk
    feeding the hungry masses
        there should be an expiration date

A Tribute to Susan Wehle
Michael Sutton

My first thought when told that Susan was on Flight 3407 was denial. But, as the realization sank in, the event went from a faceless/nameless crash to one that became very personal. It all felt rather surreal and dreamlike. Susan had been a student of mine for over four years. This couldn't be happening. I would no longer be able to look out at my students and see Susan in the front row, a bit to my right, soaking up every word, moving through each posture, sharing the Hebrew version to the Sanskrit one I offered, or providing a scriptural reference from her Jewish teachings that would very appropriately coincide with a Yoga story I had been telling. She was my most philosophic student with an intellectual capacity that spawned endless hours of conversation between us. As a matter of fact, the best classes were some of the smallest. That is, it would be Susan, another student, and my self. When that rare occasion would happen, Susan and I would just look at each other, knowing we were about to enter into a conversation that would take us beyond the normal scope that a larger class brought. We reveled in these few and far between precious times.

Since beginning yoga, Susan regularly attended my classes. She found that she could get away and be quiet within for 75 minutes a few times each week. That silence gave her the energy she needed to do the work she was called to do. Only a week and a half ago, on Friday, January 30, at the very end of our class, she said to me: "the reason I keep coming and scheduling my time around these classes is because I find such peace here. It's the only tranquility that I can seem to find."

And yet, she found tranquility in giving to others. If you knew her, you would know that if she hadn't been on that plane, she would have driven to Clarence Center to offer her help. She was one of those rare people who would give and then give some more. She lived her life fully and thrived on helping others. She used to tell me stories of these adventures, her purpose, and it was quite obvious by her passionate re-telling that she loved what she did.

I was fortunate to have her as a student for a number of reasons, chief among them when my mother became ill and eventually passed. Susan would visit my mom in the hospital singing songs in both Hebrew and English which would attract the attention of anyone walking by the room. She always had a crowd milling around my mom's hospital room at the conclusion of one of her songs. Everyone wondered where this beautiful voice was coming from. My mom, an Irish Catholic, listened to Susan's CD containing Jewish songs endlessly for the last six months of her life. At the burial site Susan sang the most hauntingly beautiful rendition of 'Amazing Grace'...her voice piercing each one of us.

Although yoga is not competitive, Susan and I would always try to outdo the other when chanting OM, the Creative Sound in the Yogic tradition. We would both start at the same time, but try as I might, I could not chant as long as she could...her voice clearly shining as she continued her song while I was already inhaling to regain my breath and begin the next OM.

Not everyone knows that Susan was an aspiring actress many years ago and actually did a milk commercial at one point. But, things that didn't work as planned changed the course of her life. We are all so fortunate for that change.

I learned of Susan's transition as I made my way home the following morning after attending a yoga class in Rochester. It was a voicemail from someone I trust and knew would have her facts correct. But I called her back anyway, asking if she was sure. She was certain. I then called a friend who is related to Susan, figuring she was already privy to the news, but realized by the lightness in her voice that she had not yet been told. I informed her of what I knew...not what I had called to do. She too was disbelieving, asking if I had any confirmation. Informing me that she was going to double check, she called back within minutes with the confirmation she had hoped she would not receive.

I began notifying others. The sentiment was the same: disbelief, incredulity, a sense of "No, no, no! Not Susan." I found my self talking to her while driving, telling her I love her, that I miss her already, telling my self that it's all a dream, that I can rewind the last 12 hours and undo all of this. In the next instant, I told her to continue helping others...from the other side. A day later, I find that I'm still talking to her.

For as close as we were, as amazing as our conversations were, I'm left feeling as though it wasn't enough.

I miss you, Susan.

Note: We honored Susan at Monday morning's 9:30 am yoga class on February 16, 2009, with prayer, chanting, and a yoga practice. Her sons, Jonah and Jake, were present.

Susansong, Enigma, and Stones—Three Poems

Rev. Gail M. Lewis

Susansong

there is a photo on my shelf

you, in your tallit, with bouncy hair,

I, in my stole, not quite so gray as now

standing with our colleagues

at once among and against them

we smile silently

the only picture I have of us

together

there is a video where you sing

the very last time

we were together

but it remains in the box

a memory too poignant to disturb

your life is more than memories

greater than the sight or sound

that has since disappeared

it is an energy that sustains us all

in each present moment

and the next

transcending time

it whispers to our hearts

a Susansong

and we learn to sing

again

Enigma

Where shall we go?

To lunch, of course!

To talk, to laugh, to cry, to shout,

To share our secrets.

You told me I had a Jewish soul.

I wonder how you knew?

Stones

I'd never left a stone before.

I'd never had a reason

or a need.

So I had no idea

that stones

could cry.

Susansong, adapted into a pendant by Rick Ellis of Temple Beth Am

Thoughts
Rabbi Irwin A. Tanenbaum, D.D.

As read by Rabbi Harry Rosenfeld, Friday, February 13, 2009, during Erev Shabbat Services at Temple Beth Am:

Marta and I share the heartbreak of this still unbelievable tragedy. Our Shabbat will be spent flying home to you. We will be with you as soon as the airplane can bring us back to be together and cry and mourn, but remember and be grateful for all that our friend and my colleague has given to us.

The community's Shabbat joy can't possibly be as complete without her presence, but we will forever hear in our inner ears, her glad songs of joyous praise, and her celebration and humanity, driving together to bring peace to our world.

Later this coming week we will gather again to more formally and properly remember Susan.

Shabbat Shalom.

From: Irwin Tanenbaum
Date: January 10, 2010 9:22:14 PM EST
To: Gunilla Kester

How about that! I have a copy of Susan's last message to the congregation . . .

Some Thoughts on the Mi Shebeirach Prayer
Cantor Susan Wehle

As Published in the March 2009 Temple Topics:

Mi Shebeirach means "the One who blessed." What a strange way to start a prayer! When we pray for healing, we want to make sure that our prayer is heard. Are we alone worthy of having our prayers heard and answered? Well, just in case we're not, we pray in the name of our ancestors. We ask that the One who blessed our foremothers and forefathers, consider their merit, and because of their worthiness, find us worthy too.

And what is this healing that we are praying for? When the person we are praying for has a broken ankle, it makes sense to pray that the ankle will heal. But how do we pray for a person that we and the doctors know is dying? I had a teacher, Rabbi Susan Gulag, who suggested that our task is to put our prayer out into the universe with all the kavannah or passionate intention we can muster, and then back off, allowing God to answer our prayer in whatever way it needs to be answered. Part of the "art" of praying requires us to have enough faith in the Divine Energy of the universe, to be able to let go of control over the outcome of our prayer. We need to believe that the best healing for this particular person may not be what we had imagined. This person's healing may require leaving his or her physical body behind. So we pray that our love and God's love merge to allow the unfolding to take place exactly as it is meant to.

There is a story about a little girl who prayed to God with every ounce of her being for a bicycle for her birthday. Her parents were concerned because they could not afford to buy her what she wanted, and feared that she might lose her faith in God. Her birthday came and went without the bicycle. When they asked her if she still believed in God after her prayer was not answered, she said, "My prayer was answered. The answer was NO!"

Our prayers are powerful, whatever the response. Praying helps us feel connected to the Divine Flow. The very act of praying is healing to us and, according to scientific research, to those for whom we pray.

Mi Shebeirach, may the One who blessed our ancestors, bless us too, with faith, with hope and with love.

Her Sisters' Eulogies for Susan Alice Wehle
With a Postscript, Poetry, Testimony, and a Memorial Reading
Dana Wehle and Eva Friedner

Dana:

If Sue were here she would listen with eager ears and compassionate heart to how we are all doing. For my part I'd say to her, I am moving in and out of solitary mourning and despair *and* profound connection with others who share the loss. Now 15 days after your and the others' horrifying deaths, I struggle to reconcile this human tragedy, the private loss of you my sister and closest friend, and the loss of you as a beloved public figure. The finality of your death now exists in stark contrast to the movement of heart, mind and soul of all of us who love and value you so. Treasured mother, sister, aunt, relative, colleague, spiritual community leader, cantor and friend, I say

> Hello my sister!
>
> Hello my sister!
>
> These words our ongoing greeting.
>
> I say to you … still
>
> Hello my sister!

Do you see the rainbow catching Ma and Da's tearful gaze as they first heard your soul and song as cantor; the beauty of Jonah and Jake whom you nurtured with brilliance and who so clearly carry your spirit in their own rights; the private world of our childhood.

Fifty years ago or so, we invented games and language while Ma shopped. You called me Milo. I called you Mila. Czech names we imitated – so foreign and fun. Sliding up and down the two inch ledge at the bottom of the meat case of all places … up and down, up and down, Milo Mila Milo Mila Milo Mila – rhythm and joy in your blood even then. Why did we find it so hilarious? A tiny memory among hundreds that we loved to chomp on. And through an unbelievable journey of following your heart, you became a public figure and accomplished singer who touched the souls and funny bones of so many beyond me. I am so deeply, deeply proud.

I praise the love you shared and inspired, the scope of your accomplishments within the Jewish community and particularly your commitment to developing venues for interfaith dialogue in Buffalo. You lived your life in dialogue with faith, and what peace it brings to know that your most recent taste of life touched bliss, peace and expansion.

I thank all of you who were Sue's teachers and angels and who in turn honored her spirit, wisdom, love and song. I thank you Sue for always supporting me, for cherishing our relationship and for always being my older sister while honoring what you called my wisdom even so, for being my spiritual teacher. I thank you for the laughter, tears, love and profound conversation during our visit less than two months ago.

Hello, my sister! Goodbye. I love you so. I miss you so.

Eva:

My little sister Suzy . . . Carrot Top . . . Suzanka . . . Sue . . . Shoshana . . . Susan. I nicknamed you "carrot top" when you were very young because of your curly (albeit not red) hair and your cute freckles. In high school you would straighten those curls on big orange juice cans or iron them out on the ironing board. (You were so much like Annie from the musical – optimistic, upbeat and smiling!) Suzy, you were so full of energy…bubbly, talkative, animated…exploding to tell Mom or the family something new and exciting. Mom couldn't quite keep up with you, sometimes saying: "Simmer down, simmer down." (In later years you shared how much you hated that!)

Little did we all know that there might have been a larger reason for your exuberant embracing of life. You packed life into every moment; whether it was playing board games with vigorous competitive passion, singing with me at camp (and more recently at family bat mitzvahs and weddings), harmonizing with me while Dad played the piano or while we were driving in the car, dancing Israeli dances late into the night long after I had already quit from exhaustion. In hindsight I feel that you had to pack it all in because there was an unforeseeable plan for you. I remember one of many precious moments when you and I bonded with loving intensity – it was in Elat Chayim, our beloved Jewish Renewal retreat center. It was in preparation for Shabbat (the Sabbath). Experiencing a communal women's mikveh (ritual bath) – my very first time and our first time together in this setting. We sang and blessed each other. We looked deeply into each other's eyes. We were so so close in our love for each other and our common Jewish connection. Thank you for that memory. I also cherish beyond words, the hot tub ceremony you orchestrated for my 60th birthday. Suzy, two days ago your wonderful boys, their loving girlfriends, Dana, and I stood together in your kitchen in a loving circle. You were palpably missing! But . . . I felt the presence of Shechinah, her wings holding and embracing us while we tried to comprehend your death. And I felt so strongly that you had become part of those embracing wings. Even though you have been taken from us – so suddenly – so rudely – in your too brief life, you have left us with eternal ripples of your love, laughter, compassion and spirit.

I love you so much! Our love pours out to you.

Eva's Postscript:

In a few weeks it will be a year since you were taken from us. So much has happened, but you know that. So I have not even truly begun to mourn you in that deep soulful way, but you have been in my consciousness and heart a lot these last few weeks. I know you understand that I have had to focus on Tamar these past few months. But now, I look at your smiling face in a picture and am receiving fresh pangs of missing you and the disbelief is returning. One year? How can that be? Come back. I need you. I miss you. Thank you for sending Tamar her healing in answer to our 'conversation' during Yom Kippur. Perhaps it is you who are orchestrating this miracle! The sparkles of light from above are falling all around us! Bless you, my sister.

And poetry from Dana:

Wicked Moment   3/7/09

Wicked moment took my sister

I am a sibow

    a widswib

    a widosib

Turn to the two precious ones

And watch them forward

Live them forward.

Your delicious boys.

Oh my sister

Wicked wicked moment

When your body, psyche, cells, pores, breath bled

with no tincture of homeopathic remedy to stop the metastasis of pain.

Ohm 3/7/09

Deep deep in the enclosed tunnel of my Ohm mouth

I see you frozen in the moment of terror.

Let us not forget that

Let us not put this burden on you to hold.

I have it, Sue

I have it.

Yes, we each had our roles and mine is to hold the pain till it turns into love and striving.

I cannot offer you chariots pulled by Eliezer

That is for others to give you and each other in soothing lullaby.

I do know I have no doubt at all

That you are part of Ohm

There you are for me

In Ohm

I will find you and know you are right there.

Pure spirit now.

Ma and Da

Tired spirits when they left

Yours full of life

The vibrations that you add to the energy of all we breathe are vital.

And with theirs too powerful for words.

I hope you are not sad

Please let that be my, our task.

Rest now my sister.

"I have never felt closer or safer with you," we shared

On January 16, 2009

I thank you so.

The Last of the Mohicans 3/8/09

No out.

I lost my sister.

Was it cancer?

No, it was a plane crash.

That's ridiculous.

No, it's true.

No out.

I lost my sister.

Do you hear me?

I am calling out to you but the sound is silent.

Widow, no.

Orphan, no.

Sisters 15 months apart our whole lives.

What happens now?

I will not see 15 months ahead at every moment.

My lifelong gauge of age no longer exists within lived time.

In that way, an orphan.

The curtain closes, but the story is not over.

The soundtrack of *The Last of the Mohicans* plays.

This is an epic story.

No Words 6/27/09

In the end we are alone.

The force of constant change in the universe is humbling.

It is impossible that Sue was on earth and now she is not.

Dear Sue,

"Hello, my sister," I can hear you sing out.

In the dark back room

The fed ex envelope with the secure pin to your found belongings lies unopened.

From "Hello, my sister"

to hair on a pink comb that they say is yours.

I hear you say,

"Dahn, do it when you are ready."

I will try to escape in a story,

Or in a movie.

You were so good at that.

It separated us too

No, I will never abandon you.

My sweet sweet Sue, it hurts so bad.

It is not your fault

It just is.

Touching the tangible will touch you as you ended.

26 seconds

There are no words

The fed ex envelope sits and stares . . .

Poor Girl 8/9/09

Impossible

Completely impossible

Da … about Alice

   Pooooor Girl

   Pooooor Girl

Susan Alice, my sister

Now you

His tender voice cries

      Pooooor Girl

Until the Task is Done 8/23/09

I will hold you close Sue

I will hold you

with a lullaby.

But now I have a job to do.

I must look at your things

charred

perhaps torn

perhaps not

perhaps so new looking it will make no sense.

You appreciate that

and still

want to do it yourself.

But now you must rest, you are resting now.

These things are from another lifetime.

They are not now.

They will warp time.

I must see them in the present and remember that the pain is over.

Your pain, my dear dear sister, is over.

My pain?

The items?

How do I detach from them?

I hum like Mama Collins.

I just hum.

I rock

I sing an old Negro spiritual while I watch you hanging from the tree

this time with no racism but equally as ugly with corporate greed.

So random.

I will hum away the anger.

I will hum until the task is done.

I will hum.

Before the House Aviation Subcommittee, September 23, 2009

Sue and I shared private jokes and language that stem back to the days when we shared a room as kids. Even with the super heavy load she carried as an adult, she always made time to read drafts of my writing, often helping me articulate and develop my ideas, fine-tuning my language and earning the privilege of making fun of what I felt to be a deep thought. I am near frozen now as I need to complete a work in progress that we had discussed many times, no longer able to turn to Sue for her astute and poetic mind, her love and encouragement, her ability to challenge and support me at once. My tears break through the ice as I hear and see us laughing and sharing together . . . knowing this will be no more.

Reading - Forest Lawn Cemetery Memorial, November 8, 2009

My oldest memories seem to evoke the fullest presence of my sister's absence. There were two of us in the tub, giggling splashing so many life times ago . . . my fellow splasher and so much more is now gone. We are grandmothers, mothers, wives, sisters, daughters, daughter-in-laws, sister-in-laws, mother-in-laws, nieces, cousins, grandfathers, fathers, husbands, brothers, sons, son-in-laws; brother-in-laws, father-in-laws, nephews, and friends who are family. In sharing this burial and memorial, we together hold the heavy shadow, the aloneness that strikes out with venom when the absence is met head on. This is the loss. We also hold the rush of warmth when under the spell of illusion, imagination, memory or more, our fallen angels come to us in sight, sound, touch, feel or smell as only they could. With the breath that forms our oneness today, we hold our 50 precious souls—together and apart, and say goodbye to each – slowly and again. With our new family, we honor their names and live our lives in celebration of theirs. This is the hope. Oh my sister . . . oh to all whom we are burying, we cherish your gifts to us, thank you for receiving our love, and gratefully pray for the peace of your sweet sweet souls. For every language, religion, culture, race we represent, the wetness of our tears and our love for those we mourn are sweetly one.

Kristin Marie Safran

July 5, 1971 – February 12, 2009
37 years, 7 months, 7 days

Cindi Saltzgiver

Bright and beautiful, kind and generous, much too young to leave this world, Kristin Marie Safran had dreams yet to come true, hopes yet to fulfil, and accomplishments yet to achieve. She didn't have the chance to grow old with her loving husband, or to see her two young daughters grow up, marry, and have children of their own. Her life was well lived, but she had so much more to give.

I always have been and always will be so very proud to be Kristin's Mom. She was a beautiful baby, a loving and giving child, an active and involved teenager and college student, and a remarkable young woman who will forever be in our hearts.

Kristin will be remembered by family, friends, and co-workers for her friendly smile, good nature, intelligence, and leadership abilities. She was an amazing person, a wonderful friend who touched so many lives in so many positive ways. She was always the one on the cheerleading squad with a big smile. Like sunshine, she brightened up a room when she stepped inside it. It was a refreshing experience to work alongside someone who was not only a brilliant professional woman, but also conscientious mother.

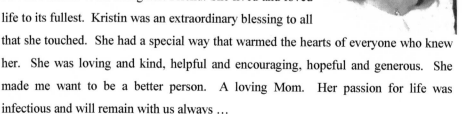

Engaged, engaging, enthusiastic, dedicated, problem-solver. Mother. Wife. Daughter. Friend. She lived and loved life to its fullest. Kristin was an extraordinary blessing to all that she touched. She had a special way that warmed the hearts of everyone who knew her. She was loving and kind, helpful and encouraging, hopeful and generous. She made me want to be a better person. A loving Mom. Her passion for life was infectious and will remain with us always …

We miss her so much, every second, every minute, every hour, every day.

From Kristin's Poetry Journal *(Submitted by her husband, Russel Safran)*

The following I found in a journal from high school or college. At the end she wrote: "These poems should be essays, 'attempts' not poems. They are rough and unpolished thoughts with at times no direction. That's why they represent me. I myself am rough and unpolished with no direction. I know they're not masterpieces or even "good." They are just what I feel." *—Kristin Saltzgiver*

My Friend
Kristin Marie Safran (nee Saltzgiver)

Through the good times
and through the bad
When I was happy
when I was sad
I always knew
If I ever needed you
You'd always be there
My friend
There's been times of laughter
and times of tears
We've gone through it all
over the years
We'll never be apart

Cause you're in my heart
And you'll always be
My friend
And now it's time when
We take different roads
I've got to prove
I can stand on my own
Though I may be by myself
I'll never be alone
Cause you'll always be with me
(you are a part of me)
My friend

The Void
Jessica Marie Safran

While I feel the void and the heartache that come with losing someone who means so much—more than anything, I feel grateful. I feel blessed to have had someone so extraordinary, so bright, so undeniably incredible to call family—and friend. She lived passionately, loved unconditionally, and knew how to laugh at herself. She was exceptionally brilliant and hard working. She fit 72 hours of life into a 24-hour day and never, not once, was she too busy to help other people. It is so uplifting to be around someone as compassionate, as light-hearted and enthusiastic as she was. I feel like she made me—makes me—a better person by association alone. She inspires me. To believe in myself. To work hard. To push myself. To always do more and to be better. To do what is right and to always make the time to help others. To make the most of life in spite of its hardship. I will keep with me all of her advice, memories of who she was and how I want to be. I hope I make her proud. Kristin, I wrote a message—printed on latex, filled with helium, and sent to the heavens. If you didn't get it: Thank you for everything.

The Safran Family

I Will Not Let You Go

Mac I. Barnett

I will not let you go, Susan. I will not allow your love for life and even more, your love for Judaism to be swallowed by the earth's crust of a burning airplane.

For me, I entered Temple Beth Am openly saying to you that I did not enjoy your singing, your high pitched voice or even the attempts to add bongo drums to the Friday night services. Having been raised in a Jewish Conservative/Orthodox lifestyle, I wanted the traditional baritone voice emanating from the bimah. I had come to Temple Beth Am for the sake of my son's Bar Mitzvah and eventually met you who changed my life even though I resisted over and over again to hear your voice call out to me.

A few years ago I joined your Service Leadership Class with the belief that my previous experiences of being a temporary chazzan in my youthful days would add to the enjoyment of attending every Friday night service. Our class of extremely diverse people melded into a 'family' of lay people who rose to the occasion of actually leading a Friday night service and experiencing the thrill of a grateful number of congregants who provided all of us with praise and encouragement for what we accomplished. We became disciples of you, your desire for continual progress with our singing, and your vast interpretation of the dynamics of what was really happening during the Seder. Even though I sang with an Ashkenazi dialect, it was you who allowed me to be me and still feel connected to the thrill of celebrating this Seder through your teaching. I gained tremendous respect for your abounding energy to help us through the tough spots, your compassionate challenge toward excellence in how we were saying the prayers, and your wisdom to connect all of our individual past experiences to the interpretation of the Friday night service; we felt as though we had been through a two year graduate training program in the several weeks that we practiced with you! We no longer just sang the words; we enjoyed the deep feeling of each sound that helped us connect to being Jewish! Singing became like praying twice – once for the words and their meaning and the second time for the thrill of feeling each sound and how it breathed life into the celebration of being Jewish!

I was amazed at your courage to accept my differences while still keeping true to your beliefs of an egalitarian lifestyle for women in the Jewish religion. I had a lot of personal challenges within the Reform movement of Temple Beth Am and you were the one person who encouraged me to take more risks toward enjoying Judaism while still clutching onto many traditions that were part of my remembrances as a child. You helped us start a Bikkur Cholim, helping the sick, group that visited people who were in need of feeling accepted and actually provided us with a contemporary course in pastoral counseling; an hour with you was exhausting but breath-taking in its revelation of what we could do as lay people for the Temple. We were creating a booklet of faith and hope that would be a part of our Temple's outreach program that would include your recorded songs. We still have some unfinished pages to complete...with your help!

I will not let go of what you've helped create within me. I believe that I am a better person for having allowed you to touch my life and I accepted your hugs as a continual blessing toward being Jewish at Temple Beth Am.

Remembering Jerry Krasuski

Justine Krasuski

I lost my husband Jerry (Jerome) on Continental Connection Flight 3407. Jerry was 53 and a program manager for Northrup Grumman, a defense contractor located in Amherst, N.Y. Jerry had just graduated in May 2007 with an MBA from the University at Buffalo School of Management, quite an accomplishment for someone 51. We were all so proud of him. There is a memorial fund at the UB School of Management and a beautiful bench with a plaque in the hall where he attended many if not all of his classes. There was even a ceremony dedicating the bench, which was presented by his classmates. I attended with just about my entire family. Jerry would have been so honored to have had an impact on so many lives.

Jerry was on business trip at an Army base in New Jersey and was returning home that night. He called me from the tarmac as I pulled into the short term parking space in the airport. When either of us went out of town, the other always parked and went inside to welcome the traveler home. As a matter of fact I had been out of town a couple of months earlier, and when Jerry picked me up from the airport, he came inside and greeted me with a rose. That night he told me he would be delayed for 45 minutes to an hour. We said. "I love you," and I went back home to await his phone call when he landed. I started watching a movie that was not on a local channel, so I was unaware of the plane crash until my cousin called after 11:00 p.m. and asked if Jerry had called me yet to pick him up. When I said, "No," she told me to turn on the local news channel. That is how I found out the plane had crashed and at that moment my body turned to jelly, even though I still did not know that it was his flight. When I finally heard it was Flight 3407, I went numb and my whole world fell apart.

Jerry was a wonderful husband, father and provider. Most of all he was my protector and friend. We have one beautiful daughter, Stacy, and a son-in-law,

Larry. Jerry was proud and honored to walk her down the aisle at her wedding, and four months before the end of Jerry's life, we became grandparents for the first time, when Stacy and Larry gave us our granddaughter, Ava. Jerry was thrilled to be a grandfather. He even bought her a pink baseball mitt, one month before he died. He could hardly wait to play with her and teach her everything he knew—which would have been something to see because we used to call him "The Walking Encyclopedia."

On all the holidays and family occasions there is now an emptiness that just won't go away. I wake up alone and go to sleep alone. On Christmas I woke up to an empty house. That feeling crushed me as no other ever had.

Jerry and I would have been married 29 years in May 2009 and would have been together for 32 years. I miss the date nights, which we tried to do one weekly. I miss the trips to fill up his gas tank or to go to Home Depot—he would bribe me with a coffee just so I would go with him. We would walk the mall hand in hand, even if we did not buy anything. Whenever we could be, we were together. He had a very busy and stressful job, but *always* found time to call me a couple times a day, just to see how I was and what we were going to do that night. We used to laugh because he called me so much. Now the phone does not ring. I worked only five minutes away from him and if he could fit lunch into his schedule, we would meet for a fast bite. Thank goodness, we met for lunch the day he left for New Jersey. That was the last meal we ate together.

Thank goodness for my daughter, son-in-law, and granddaughter, and for friends and family, all of whom have been great and a big help to me. I don't know what I would do without them. But at the end of each day my heart is once again empty and I miss Jerry so much that it is almost unbearable. And I often wonder what he was feeling and thinking those last seconds. I can't even imagine. That night will stay with me and haunt me forever. All the plans we had that will never be, all the times that will no longer be shared. And I think, *This all could have been avoided.*

I have found some peace with the Families of 3407. They are a wonderful group of people who truly understand, who have dealt with and still are dealing with this tragedy. They are a great comfort to me and my family. They will always be a part of my life and I am proud to be a part of trying to make changes in the safety, training, and fatigue issues for pilots and the commercial and regional air carriers so future air passengers can all be safer.

I must thank all of Western New York for their thoughts, prayers, contributions and help through this awful tragedy that has affected everyone. And to the first responders, I must offer a special thank you.

Jerry will always be in our hearts, thoughts, and prayers. We love him and will miss him, always.

The Krasuski Family and Jerry's Graduation

From Pilot Control

Larry Sicurella

This is pilot control, Flight 3407,

the weather looks fine as we now enter heaven

We had a safe flight, though we did come in late

When we depart from the plane, there's St. Peters gate

The Lord just informed me of prayers sent to heaven

They were sent by the loved ones of flight 3407

We took a small detour, but there's nothing to fear

The Lord will make sure we're all safe up here

We see churches full, as loved ones say their goodbyes

We see sadness and tears in every ones eyes

To each father, mother, husband and wife

"Be happy for us, and go on with your life"

Though we're no longer with you, we'll never be apart

As long as the memories are still in your heart

That's our gift to you as our Lord shows the way

He assures that we'll all be together some day

Our legacy lives on in each one of you

So encourage our children in whatever they do

Put on your best smile and don't be depressed

It's amazing up here, there's no wind or ice

There's a beautiful garden in Paradise

There's so much to tell you, but there is this one thing

Please remember us in worship or whenever you sing

Know that we're always thinking of you

And know we're beside you in whatever you do

Though it's time to sign off from flight 3407

Remember us always. We'll be smiling from heaven.

A Voice for Healing:
Remembering the Unique Song of Cantor Susan Wehle

Rabbi Irwin A. Tanenbaum

Special to *The Jewish Week*

She had a song in her heart. And she carried that song with her, from Purim parties to Yizkor services to hospital beds, along the way touching countless Jewish Buffalonians.

What do I see when I remember Susan Wehle, my friend and colleague? I see her magnificent full-face smile and bouncing curly hair. I see her amazing cheerfulness in almost all circumstances. I see her vibrant in costume during Purim, so very joyful during Shabbat, so involved before a class of adults or students. I see her walking with an arm around a youngster earnestly sharing a quiet moment.

What do I hear when I listen with my inner ear? I hear her prayerful songs of praise. I hear her joyful children's ditties. I hear her soulful hymns extolling God's greatness and glory. I hear her touching, poignant "Eil Mole" at funeral and Yizkor services.

What do I treasure when I think of Susan? I treasure that she loved our people and our God. I treasure that she cherished each moment spent in rapture before the Almighty, wrapped in her beautiful tallit, swaying slowly in the moment. I treasure that Susan cared for God's great world and reveled in its beauty and bounty. I treasure her animated personality, her *joie de vivre*.

Her zest and her spirit touched one and all.

Our Talmud teaches us that "the loss of a single person is like the destruction of an entire world." Susan's life encompassed many worlds. She gave her heart and soul to them all, never holding back.

She loved the world of her family: her two sons, Jonah and Jacob Mink, her siblings Eva Friedner, John Wehle, and Dana Wehle. Our hearts grieve for them and with them. May they know some small measure of consolation because of her unflinching love for them. She has joined the celestial realm, and it is they who must remain with their pain and loss, until they are joined more fully again.

Susan loved the world of her congregation, Temple Beth Am, a member of the Union for Reform Judaism, and before that Temple Sinai, a Reconstructionist shul. To these holy congregations she devoted her considerable energies and spirit, her love and concern. She came to us when we were weary or ill to lift our spirits by her presence and her soft songs of healing and prayer. She taught our children and enriched our adults.

Cantor Wehle gave of herself with a unique sense of the spirit within, infused by the presence of God. She taught us that life is a journey, and with music and prayer, dance and poetry, she helped us navigate. Nothing was too small or too large for her to do for us. She cannot be replaced in our hearts.

Susan loved the world of the community. She eagerly embraced projects and committees both in our Jewish community and along the broader road of all humanity. She dared to hope. She worked with The Holocaust Resource Center, her awareness heightened by memories of her survivor parents .

She forged new inroads among suburban teenagers from Jewish and Muslim families. Susan had a unique style of visiting hospitals and nursing homes, singing her way into hearts and souls. (Her CD, "Songs of Healing and Hope," is very popular). She embodied the ideal of "a light unto the nations."

Susan loved The Aleph Jewish Renewal Movement. Her many friends there shared her worldview, alive with the breath of the Almighty. With them she studied and learned, danced and sang, and thereby worshipped the Creator. With them she was ordained a cantor under the auspices of Rabbi Zalman-Schacter-Shalomi in 2004.

Our own world is a darker place now for want of her illumined soul. Her presence among us is now a void, and we must be satisfied by her memory alone, and our own ability to emulate and follow her mighty example of living life in its fullest.

Susan Wehle knew deep in her soul's inner recess that at the root of all there surely could be found that ever-enfolding embrace of Adonai our God — and she does now abide warm and safe therein.

Shiru l'adonai shir hadash, Sing unto God a new song. (Psalm 96:1)

Sing on, dear friend, you will sing on forever.

Zichronah Livracha — May her memory truly be for a blessing.

In Remembrance of Lorin Maurer

Scott Maurer

"It's a beautiful day, and it is great to be alive"—that is the motivating phrase that hung over the mirror in my daughter's bedroom the four years she attended Rowan University to complete her undergraduate studies in Exercise Science and Health Fitness. When she went to the University of Florida to complete her Masters degree in Sports Management, she again hung this phrase above the doorway from her bedroom. This slogan would appear three more times as a screen saver phrase streaming across the computer screen during her professional assignments with the NCAA, Mountain West Conference, and finally Princeton University. Not every day is a beautiful day but my daughter believed her favorite phrase was the only way to begin each day if you want to be successful, motivated, and happy. And if your day does drift toward the many challenges we all face in life, then anchor yourself in this slogan and chances are you will be more focused on the good things in life versus those that can get you down.

Lorin celebrated her 30th birthdayDecember 28, 2008. During the Christmas holiday of that year she shared with our family that the relationship with her boyfriend Kevin Kuwik had become serious. Her exact words were, "I can see myself spending the rest of my life with Kevin." Since this had come from a woman who had put most of her young adult life on hold to pursue her dream of becoming a Division I Athletic Director, we knew she was in love. Although she lived in Princeton, New Jersey, and Kevin in Indianapolis, Indiana, they never went more than a few weeks apart without meeting someplace to spend time together.

February 12, 2009 was to be such a rendezvous and was intended to be the start of a very romantic weekend in Buffalo, New York. Kevin's brother Keith was getting married on Valentines Day and Kevin would be the Best Man. Lorin was going to meet the entire Kuwik family for the first time. She was very excited about this trip and bought a special dress to wear for the occasion.

That evening, after she boarded Continental Flight 3407 at Newark airport, high winds resulted in a delay for safety. While the plane waited on the tarmac for the weather to improve, Lorin and Kevin texted each other about the snow, ice, and cold weather. Lorin was not fond of cold weather, and Kevin took the opportunity to tease her about the normal winter conditions for Buffalo at this time of the year.

Finally after several hours of waiting for the winds to subside, Continental Flight 3407 took off for Buffalo. Less than 60 minutes after take off 50 lives were lost, and our family and Kevin will never see Lorin again. The world as we knew it was changed forever. My wife will not know the excitement of helping her daughter select that perfect wedding dress. I will not get to walk her down the aisle to give her away in marriage. And worst of all, Lorin lost the opportunity to live a full, normal life and experience the joy of raising a family, as we did. The terrible tragedy of 3407 took all that and more from us.

It is unnatural for parents to bury their children. The days, weeks, and months since the accident have been mixed with emotions. Right now virtually every activity of our daily lives causes us to think of Lorin and what might have been. Families of previous fatal airline accidents tell us that this will lessen but never go away. We are working very hard to anchor our thoughts and lives in the slogan that Lorin used for so many years to take a negative and turn it into a positive. And so I say to you with the love of my daughter hanging on every word, "It's a beautiful day, and it is great to be alive."

Flight After 3407

Sinéad Tyrone

I

It always amazes me
when these big metal birds of manmade creation
transport themselves across the barriers,
into the realms of sun and cloud You created.
The clouds look so different
seen from Your vantage point,
the sun so brilliant,
the clouds like giant cotton balls,
nothing of human origin to blemish or darken this view.

II

Is this what you saw
on your final flight?
Clouds above world,
floating below you,
nothing but metal
between you and God?
But no,
your flight was at night.
Did you see the stars,
or the moon?
You had no way of knowing
that soon you would join that other world,
where no barriers exist between God and you,

where you can see moon and stars

side by side with the Creator.

How grateful I am

that your agony was short,

that in almost no time

you were home for eternity,

safe for all time.

III

There are no boundaries

when flying above the clouds,

no countries or states,

no fences,

no politics.

The only language we speak is prayer.

Keep us safe,

O God.

Ride with us.

Land us gently.

Inventory: All But One

Gunilla Theander Kester

One of the few

One on a rope

One to a gun

One between angels

One with her words

One into holy space

One near the desert

One at your well

One after rain

One beside herself

One until change

One without wine

One for a voice

One during another

One despite sand

One since the flood

One among birds

One about stones

One up the mountain

One through the sword

One beyond hope

One in a wind

One by a crown

One toward peace

One from a saint

One across town

One as a beast

One outside reach

One over stars

One like a dog

One above numbers

One before dreams

One except pain

One within joy

One against many

One below grade

One under threat

One upon thought

One behind masks

One around books

One along songs

One beneath trees

One off of herbs

The ring of sorrow

carves a hole

we all share

differently

Let us Amen

Let us Shalom

Contributors

Peter Breitsch is the former pastor of Trinity Lutheran Church.

Mac I. Barnett is a member of Temple Beth Am.

Rachel Fix Dominguez is a former student of the Bennett Park Montessori Center and a friend of the family of Alison Des Forges.

Alexa Draman is an 8th grade student in Williamsville. She had just completed her Bat Mitzvah studies with Cantor Susan Wehle at the time of the tragedy.

Eva Friedner is Susan Wehle's sister.

Andrew Gold is a Maggid (itinerant preacher and skilled storyteller) and Rabbinic Pastor, and leads a contemplative Jewish community in Santa Fe. He is also the director of an inter-traditional retreat center in the mountains of northern New Mexico.

Judy Henn teaches Religious School and serves as Vice President of Worship at Temple Beth Am, Williamsville, NY. She has been a WNY interior designer for the past 25 years.

Linda Hirschhorn is a singer/songwriter/composer/cantor. Her latest recording is the CD *Becoming* (www.lindahirschhorn.com).

Barbara D. Holender is a well-known Western New York poet and writer.

Michelle Kearns is a *Buffalo News* Staff Reporter.

Gunilla Theander Kester, award-winning poet and the author of *Time of Sand and Teeth*, teaches classical guitar at the Amherst School of Music.

Justine Krasuski is the wife of Jerome (Jerry) Krasuski.

Jennifer Lee lives near the crash site and took on-scene photos of first responders.

Laura Masters is in her senior year at Denison University as an English Creative Writing major and is completing her first collection of stories. She grew up in WNY.

Scott Maurer is the father of Lorin Maurer.

Marge Merrill is Director of Medical Records for the Total Aging in Place program of the Weinberg Campus. Her poetry has appeared in the debut issue of *Beyond Bones*.

Jay L. Mesnekoff, president of Mesnekoff Funeral Home, lives in Clarence Center and enjoys the outdoors, sports, landscaping, music, and community and religious activities.

Jonah Mink, an accomplished photographer, is Susan's Wehle's oldest son and studies medicine in Israel.

Barbara D. Miller is an Associate Professor of Spanish at Buffalo State College.

Marek P. Parker is a Buffalo-based poet, fiction writer and special education teacher. (www.buffalome.com/profile/MarekPparker)

Gary Earl Ross, a language arts professor at the UB EOC, is the author of the Edgar Award-winning play *Matter of Intent* and the 2009 historical novel *Blackbird Rising.*

Jane Sadowsky is an administrative assistant at the Stanley G. Falk School. Her poetry can also be found in *Beyond Bones.*

Cindi Saltzgiver is the mother of Kristin Marie Safran.

Russel and **Jessica Marie Safran** are the husband and stepdaughter of Kristin Marie Safran.

Larry Sicurella is a friend of the Krasuski family.

Sheldon Soman, a network administrator for Niagara-Wheatfield CSD, writes music and poetry in his spare time.

Michael Sutton is the founder of Rising Sun Yoga.

Irwin Tanenbaum is the rabbi at Temple Beth Am.

Sinéad Tyrone is a legal assistant residing in Cheektowaga. She is currently working on a collection of poems and a novel.

Dana Wehle is Susan Wehle's sister.

Jennifer West is the wife of 3407 victim Ernie West. She devotes herself to their three-year-old daughter, Summer Tyme, and the cause of ensuring safer air travel regulations.

Elizabeth Wheat is a Ph.D. Candidate in the Biology Department at the University of Washington.

Marianne Wisbaum married her high school sweetheart after graduating with a B. S. in English. Her passions include her husband and three daughters, holistic living, reading, traveling, the arts, writing, and volunteering for causes she believes in.

Edward G. Wright is a risk manager for the forest industry. He writes poetry, short fiction and opinion pieces when he can.

(Some contributors have chosen not to supply a biographical note and to let their words speak for them.)